BRAND THE CHANGE

B**IS**PUBLISHERS

BIS Publishers
Building Het Sieraad
Postjesweg 1 1057 DT
Amsterdam The Netherlands
T +31 (0)20 515 02 30
bis@bispublishers.com
www.bispublishers.com

ISBN 978-90-636947-8-4
Copyright © 2017 Anne Miltenburg
and BIS Publishers.
2nd printing 2018

FOR ALL THE PEOPLE FIGHTING THE GOOD FIGHT

INDEX

CHAPTER 1
BRANDING 101

What you need to know about branding before you build your own brand.

CHAPTER 2
CASE STUDIES

Fourteen changemaking organisations open up about building their brand.

CHAPTER 3
BRAND ANATOMY

We unpack the anatomy of a brand and offer inspiring examples of existing brands.

CHAPTER 4
BUILD YOUR BRAND STEP BY STEP

The brand building process explained in four phases comprised of 22 steps. Follow the steps to build your own brand, supported by our tools with examples from existing brands.

CHAPTER 5
TOOL TEMPLATES

Eleven blank tool templates for your own use.

CHAPTER 6
EXERCISES

Twelve exercises to kickstart your thinking and inspire your team.

CHAPTER 7
EXPERT TIPS AND TRICKS

Guest essays by experts.

CHAPTER 8
THE BEGINNING

INTRODUCTION

On a Tuesday night in February of 2014, I was driving home from Amsterdam to The Hague around midnight. I had just been in a 14-hour brand thinking session, and I was tired. I had been asked by a drugstore chain to come up with a compelling reason why women should choose their store over another drugstore, even though they sell exactly the same products at the same price. That's quite an intellectual challenge, but not an unusual one for a brand developer. So I had been staring at a box of tampons and a lipstick all day, trying to come up with that one great idea, and my brain was fried.

So in the car, in an attempt to distract myself, I turned on the radio, and I fell right into the story of an app that helps diagnose eye disease and prevent blindness, using any smartphone. And it made me angry! Why was I listening to this incredible story at midnight on a niche Dutch radio channel, a radio channel that had an audience of maybe 300 people at that hour? Why wasn't this on prime time TV? Why was something with so much value and relevance to all of us getting so little attention while my tampon and lipstick client could get millions of people to run to their store? And that got me thinking.

Of course there are several reasons why great ideas for social or environmental impact don't always get the attention they deserve. The first one we always think of is money, and of course big budgets can make a big difference in getting the attention of the public, but I don't believe this is the main problem. A second reason is that I often notice people assume bad products need branding, and good products just sell themselves. And I believe the third is knowledge. Many (social) entrepreneurs do not have enough knowledge about branding or access to the expertise they need to build a strong brand. Branding knowledge is dispensed by lofty branding gurus who use Apple and Coca-Cola as examples–which are totally unrealistic benchmarks for entrepreneurs starting out.

I asked myself how I can help create a world where a family starting a fair trade lemonade factory in Sierra Leone has access to the same branding knowledge as a company like Coca-Cola? In the summer of 2014, I founded The Brandling: a learning company that democratises branding knowledge and builds brand thinking skills with changemakers across the world. This book captures our method and gathers answers to the hundreds of questions we get asked in the field. The big strategic questions and small practical ones. A process from A-Z instead of abstract inspiration that stops at the point where you want to put it to use for your own end. Tips from founders who have been there.

When we are building something new, a company, a movement, a product, we hope that people are waiting for what we have to offer. We hope they will spread the word far and wide for us. Here is the bad news: no one cares. Chances are, our video won't go viral, our friends will not share our posts en masse, investors won't be clamouring at the door to get a slice of the pie. Building a brand takes blood, sweat and perhaps even a few tears. Here is the good news: your chances of success will be much better if you arm yourself with the knowledge you need to get the audiences whose support you seek.

Here's to all the changemakers who are working to create a better world for us all. I wish you the brand you deserve!

Anne Miltenburg

Find Anne on twitter: @annemiltenburg

Anne Miltenburg (1981) is a brand developer who works in places as diverse as Paris, Bamako, Seoul, Boston and Riyadh and currently calls Nairobi home. Educated as a designer at the Royal Academy of Fine Arts, Anne worked for several world-renowned branding agencies first as a designer, then as a strategist and finally as creative director. In 2014 she founded The Brandling to focus exclusively on advancing ideas, products and services for positive social and environmental change through brand thinking.

WHO THIS BOOK IS FOR

👍

JOIN THE TRIBE

In our Facebook Group readers can ask questions and exchange learnings: facebook.com/groups/brandthechange

Branding is a tool, and, like any tool, you can use it for good or evil. The intention of this book is to democratise branding knowledge to advance the progress of businesses with positive social or environmental impact.

We want to see changemaking organisations become so successful in the skill of brand thinking that they create a paradigm shift in which social and environmental good will be the new business as usual.

This book is primarily developed for the needs of...
» Social enterprises/b-corporations.
» Startups.
» Existing small to medium-sized businesses
» Teams within large organisations who want to define or strengthen their purpose.
» NGOs and charities.

However, we see a far wider function of brand thinking as a skill to advance people, movements and ideas. Brand thinking can play a large role for people looking to strengthen their leadership, or to build a community of like-minded people around a common cause.

Therefore the book will also be of use to
» Leaders
» Movements
» Activists

To avoid endless repetition of all of the types of readers listed above, we simply refer to organisations and entrepreneurs.

Know that when you read 'organisation' we mean entities of all types of sizes, sectors, structures and phases, from a one-person business to a movement of hundreds of thousands of citizens, from startups to existing large-scale operations. When you read 'entrepreneur' we can mean scientists, activists, teachers, carpenters, and all other imaginable professions. We can refer to serial business builders as well as intrapreneurs.

Creatives and brand strategists use the book to get a better understanding of how they can apply their skills for good.

LEAN APPROACH
We advocate a lean approach to brand development: co-create ideas, test them with individuals and small groups, adapt and evolve. The method described in this book does not incorporate large-scale qualitative and quantitative testing, focus group discussions and expert market research. These types of research can be inserted at any point if you want to base your work on solid data. However, for most of our readers those activities are out of reach due to budget and time restrictions and therefore we have left them out.

This book has come into existence to offer changemakers a solid grasp of the basics of branding. With it, you can create a blueprint for your brand. It will not make you a brand strategist and cannot replace a great designer or copywriter, but it will help you build your brand thinking skills, have a better understanding of the entire branding process and more confidence in your ability to build your brand for change.

WHEN TO START
THE BRANDING PROCESS

AT THE START OF YOUR THINKING AROUND YOUR NEW INITIATIVE, DURING BUSINESS MODEL GENERATION

AT THE MOMENT YOU ARE READY TO REACH OUT TO YOUR FIRST AUDIENCES (PRIVATELY OR PUBLICLY)

WHEN YOU ARE AN EXISTING ORGANISATION FACING A REPUTATION PROBLEM, A DISRUPTED MARKET OR A CONTEXT THAT HAS CHANGED

The process of distilling your mission and vision, and deciding how to translate these into tangible products, services, partnerships and places (which is a process inherent to branding), catalyses inspired thinking that helps you to re-examine, strengthen or fine-tune the concept of your business, product or service.

Branding will help you frame who you are, what you do and why it matters, and will generate ideas on who your audiences are, what you have to offer them, and how you can reach them. This is vital to investors, supporters, partners, (potential) employees, suppliers and the media, whether it is on a public, global platform or in a first pitch deck you send in a single private email. Ten years ago it would have been wise to delay investing resources in brand development until the business model had been completely set. Today, it can take startups quite a while to find the right business model, so branding becomes relevant from your first presentation to an investor, whether that is your mother or a big fund.

A major change in your industry need not be the end of your organisation. How can you reframe what you do and why it matters? Branding can help you rethink your purpose and positioning. It can also help guide you through actions that are necessary to change your reputation.

 MACMILLAN CANCER SUPPORT
A case study of an organisation which had a reputational problem and rebranded successfully.
Read it on page 42.

INVEST IN YOUR BRAND

The branding process is extensive and takes dedication and time. A strong brand is not built overnight but requires years of work.

RESPONSIBILITY AND CAPACITY

There are two types of effort needed to build a brand: the bigger-picture strategy and the day-to-day activities. For both you need good people, time and money, and you will need to reserve all three in order to make any progress.

Everyone on your team should feel they own the brand and contribute to it, but make sure there is someone on your leadership team who truly owns the brand as their main responsibility. This person is in charge of the bigger picture: creating it and adjusting it over time and engaging people with it through inspiration and strategic support.

If you have people on your team or outside agencies working to create your brand or actions and communications, they will all need to understand that bigger picture and why they do what they do. The person who owns the brand plays a crucial role, and the ideas you generate in the strategic phase will be put to practical use here.

If you are a solo entrepreneur, you will need to make a first effort to create a brand blueprint and get your visual and verbal identity up and running, but don't forget the long haul. Carve out time every two weeks to check on the bigger picture. On a weekly basis, you will also need a dedicated number of hours to either oversee brand-related activities or to make them happen yourself. Since everything stops and starts with you, keeping your brand on the radar as well as on your calendar is crucial.

A JUMP START

Of course it is possible that you purchased this book in a phase of your business where you cannot yet dedicate a substantial and consistent amount of time and resources to brand development. If you simply want to get acquainted with brand thinking, we recommend reserving a day to dive into the materials and create a rough sketch to start off with. Clear your agenda, find a space that relaxes and focuses you, close the door and clear some wallspace. Grab the following tools:

» Insight generator p. 163
» Brand Thinking Canvas 1 p. 166
» Brand Thinking Canvas 2 p. 168
» Action Planner p. 176

Hang the two Brand Thinking Canvases on the wall next to each other. To the left and the right of the canvases, add an empty flipchart sheet or large writing surface.

Use the empty sheet to the left of the Brand Thinking Canvas Part One for your insight generator and write down your brand proposition (as described in Chapter 2, Phase 1, Step 2). Use the Brand Thinking Canvas Part One and Two as directed. Finish with capturing your ideas as a list of actions on the empty sheet on the right.

RESERVING RESOURCES
See page 111 to learn more about reserving time and budget for branding.

DIGITAL VERSION

The Brand Thinking Canvas is available on
poster size at www.the-brandling.com/
brandthinkingcanvas
Download the digital version for free
by using the discount code 'bisreaders2'
at checkout.

LEGEND

Throughout this book we will use icons and colour-coded blocks. Yellow blocks are for inspiration. Black blocks are references to other content in the book, such as case studies or tools.

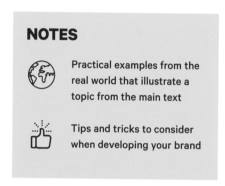

NOTES

Practical examples from the real world that illustrate a topic from the main text

Tips and tricks to consider when developing your brand

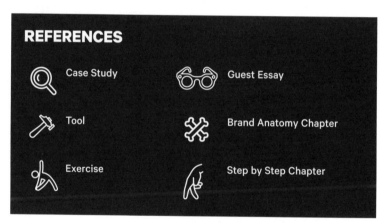

REFERENCES

Case Study

Tool

Exercise

Guest Essay

Brand Anatomy Chapter

Step by Step Chapter

CHAPTER 1
BRANDING 101

A SHORT HISTORY

Branding proclaims allegiance.

Branding makes you stand out from the crowd.

Branding advances your reputation.

Branding shows ownership.

Branding is an inherent human practice of all ages and all cultures, a way of showing who you are and what you stand for.

For ages, artists have signed their work in order to build their reputations. Silver and goldsmiths have developed marks of quality to instil trust. Knights and warriors were clad in the colours and symbols of their houses or tribes, proclaiming their allegiances, distinguishing them from the enemy, and advancing their reputations. The actual word 'branding' derives from the branding of cattle in the United States in the 19th century to show and prove ownership.

Branding as we know it today came of age during the Industrial Revolution. Large-scale production and faster logistics meant that the distance between producer and consumer grew.

Word-of-mouth was no longer effective as a single tool for spreading a reputation. Especially for food, the safety and quality of products was a big question mark. Creating more recognisable identities for their products helped manufacturers build trust and loyalty.

By the mid-20th century, most manufacturers could no longer compete based purely on quality, as most goods on the market were roughly the same. So manufacturers had to develop another differentiating factor to make products stand out on the store shelf, a more emotional appeal, and advertising, marketing and branding came into their own. Today, branding is used by individuals, governments, activists, movements, political parties, products, services, scientists and celebrities to help guide people how to think and feel about them.

BRANDING: A DEFINITION

There have been a lot of books written on branding, and experts can argue about its exact definition until they are blue in the face. For the purpose of this book, we are defining branding as directing how other people think and feel about you.

Your brand is a catalyst that drives everything you do, from your actions to your communications, from your HR policy to choosing a new location for your office. Through your actions people will (unconsciously) build an archive of associations of your brand. By being aware of what you want to be recognised for by others and designing the right actions and communications which will build that recognition, you can actively guide how other people think and feel about you.

> 'A brand is a person's gut feeling about a product, service or company. A brand is not what you say it is, it is what they say it is.' —Marty Neumeier, author

> 'Brands exist in the minds of the people who interact with them.' —Brian Collins, creative director,

BRANDING HELPS YOUR AUDIENCE

Every day we are bombarded by thousands of messages from thousands of people, organisations and products who think that we should buy them, read them, eat them, fund them. Brands help people choose. Developing a brand strategy means not leaving your audience's choice to chance, but having a plan about who you want on board to support you and how you can get them on board. You can't control it entirely, and neither should you want to, but if you don't frame how you want to be thought of, others will frame you –right or wrong– as they see fit.

BRANDING HELPS YOU

Internally, a brand provides purpose, is a compass for direction and a filter in decision making. Branding is choosing. You can't be everything to everyone. If you try to be everything to everyone you end up being nothing to nobody. A strong brand helps you take better decisions on new opportunities and creates a stronger company culture where values are shared and where actions are more aligned.

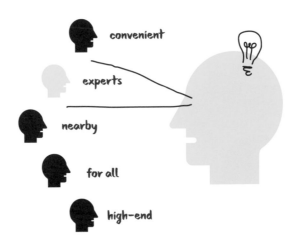

Branding helps your audience choose

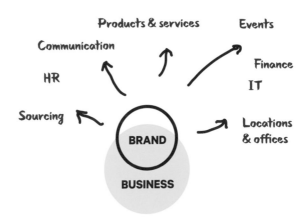

Branding helps you choose

ABN AMRO

HSBC

BNP Paribas

I NEED A BANK!
WHICH BANKS
DO I KNOW?

ING direct

ARE THEY
RIGHT FOR ME?

ABN AMRO experts in
investments, not what I'm looking
for right now

HSBC: high-end, out of my
reach

BNP Paribas: large & old
fashioned

ING Direct: online,
easy, for all

I PREFER ING DIRECT,
WHAT DO I KNOW
ABOUT THEM?

no negative reviews
found online

sponsor youth soccer in
my old eighbourhood

wasn't there
a scandal in 2008?
let me check...

Judy uses them

billboards in town
recently

YEP,
LET'S GO FOR
ING DIRECT

BRANDING IS A MIND GAME

If branding is all about directing what others think and feel about you, then it is really a mind game. Your goal: to position yourself in the mind of your audience and to have their preference. Positioning is central to branding and crucial to your success. To be considered, you need to be known. To get on someone's mental shortlist it needs to be clear what you offer and for whom. To be selected, people will run through their mental archive to check what they know about you and if that resonates with them. If they believe you are trustworthy, offer the best solution to their need and that you are aligned on values, you can beat the competition. This journey of consideration and choice is the same for consumers looking for a bank, a social impact investor looking to fund startups, a recent graduate looking for a job or a person who wants to donate half of her end of year bonus to a good cause.

COMPETITION VERSUS COLLABORATION

Positioning yourself in a market helps you to be different from other players in the same field. Social enterprises often don't like to think they are in competition. To think that not-for-profits or social enterprises don't compete is an illusion.

WE ALL COMPETE IN SOME WAY FOR TIME, ATTENTION, INVESTMENT, SALES, GRANTS, AWARDS, SPEAKER LISTS OR TALENTED EMPLOYEES

Therefore, it is important to brand yourself in a differentiating manner. And that is not just needed to be competitive: it is also needed when you want to be collaborative. To achieve a better world, we need to work together. Having a strong positioning will make that easier. When your brand and another brand have a clear complementary service, you can team up. When you have shared values and a shared audience, you can create a partnership.

 MAP OUT THE MARKET
What does your market look like and how will you position yourself? Create a market map, see page 187.

WHAT BRANDING IS NOT

In an effort to change their reputations, many people, companies and governments turn to PR and branding. If all we do is try to influence perception through communication, it is simply propaganda. Nor should we go for merely cosmetic operations. For people and operations to be believable, communication must be aligned with action.

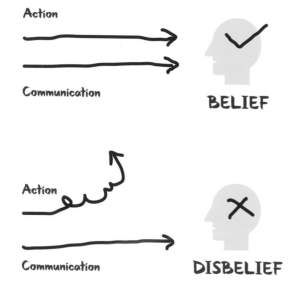

Branding is a great tool, but it does come with some dangers. Turn on your 'bullshit radar'. Be sure to test every idea and phrase against reality. Don't be afraid of sharing a bold vision, but be honest, open and transparent with what you are trying to achieve. Always make it as compelling and original as possible. Keep it simple (simple is hard). Eschew jargon.

IN ORDER TO GAIN A GOOD REPUTATION, ONE MUST ENDEAVOUR TO BE AS ONE DESIRES TO APPEAR —SOCRATES

THE BOUNDARIES OF BRANDING

Is branding marketing? Is it advertising? Is branding a logo or a video that goes viral? All the above can be part of your brand, but they are not synonymous with it. Marketing helps you to bring a product to the market. Marketeers can use point of sales material for this, or a reward programme. Advertising is usually structured around a campaign that can include ads, commercials, Facebook apps, web banners and flyers. A logo is part of your visual identity, and therefore an important part of your brand. A video that you have created can be a great medium to tell your message. All of them are part of your brand, but none encompass it.

THE BULLSHIT RADAR
Do you think you are immune to jargon, fluffy language or abstractions? Do the Bullshit Radar Exercise.
See page 193.

WHAT MAKES A STRONG BRAND?

Whether a brand is strong is not just a question of taste. A strong brand has measurable qualities. It is:

RECOGNISABLY DIFFERENT

Know what role you want to play within your market. How do you distinguish yourself from others in the same field or with similar offers? What do you want to be recognised for? Branding is choosing. Brand strategist Suzanne van Gompel takes the restaurant business as a simple example: if you position yourself as specialising in vegetarian and non-vegetarian food, you end up being nothing to no one.

BASED ON A STRONG 'WHY'

Articulating why you do what you do, to what bigger aim, will help you connect to your audiences, as well as give you a guiding principle for everything you do as an organisation. Your purpose makes your brand directional, it provides a dot on the horizon to work towards.

A STORY PEOPLE CAN RE-TELL

Build it around your mission, an insight, moment or person that led you to do what you do. Nothing builds a stronger connection between you and your audience than a story that is relevant and memorable. Stories allow your audiences to share your experience and become your ambassadors.

CLEAR IN ITS COMMUNICATION

Strong brands create clarity. You cannot expect to attract people's interest and support if they cannot understand what you offer them. This may seem too simple to mention, but you would be surprised how often organisations fail to communicate clearly what they offer. Be sure to articulate the real value for both your audience (what they get out of engaging with you) and the world (what the bigger issue is).

A LIVING BRAND

A strong brand is not just painting everything you do in a brand colour. It is about making it come alive through everything you do. Whether your audience watches you speak at a conference, visit your website, call your customer service, or attend your event, everything they encounter should live and breathe what you stand for.

HOW DO YOU SAY 'DON'T SHOOT ME' IN 350 LANGUAGES?

Strong brands trigger a lifetime of associations in the minds of an audience. In the case of the Red Cross the recognisability and memorability of their brand can literally mean the difference between life and death.

A STRONG NAME AND FACE

Don't sell yourself short with a generic brand. Create a brand identity that translates your internal character into a unique, differentiating external identity and personality.

REALISTIC AND TRUSTWORTHY

At the end of the day, the product or service that you deliver will define how people think and feel about you. When building your brand, never ever forget to walk the walk. Never over-promise and underdeliver.

WHY BRAND THE CHANGE?

In a perfect world, great ideas would spread, based purely on their own merit. But unfortunately, we do not live in a perfect world. In order to turn changemaking ideas into reality, we are going to need investors, talented employees, partners, customers or clients. And in order to convince them to come on board, we have to get really good at selling our concepts for change. Branding is the perfect method to do just that.

Building a brand is not an easy feat, but once you have made the investment into building a strong brand, it will start to do a lot of the heavy lifting for you.

It is our conviction that when changemakers get the brands they deserve, not only will their organisations do better, but by outperforming traditional businesses, we will create a paradigm shift whereby social good simply is the best way to do business.

RESEARCH HAS SHOWN THAT A STRONG BRAND...

» Can yield higher profit margins, as well as bigger financial investment and grants.
» Creates more and longer interactions with your audience.
» Builds more loyalty, referrals, and repeat business.
» Helps attract the best talent for your team.
» Helps attract better strategic partnerships.

These outcomes are exactly what social entrepreneurs need when they are working towards impact! When you are a startup, branding can help to get your first client or investor and to launch your product or service successfully. When you are an established organisation, branding can help strengthen what you have built or can bring you into a new phase when your market is disrupted, when your context changes or when your organisation experiences internal change.

BRANDS INVITE THE RECOGNITION THAT GREAT THINGS ARE USUALLY NOT DONE BY INDIVIDUALS ACTING IN HEROIC ISOLATION. AT SOME POINT EVERY GOOD IDEA, EVERY IMPORTANT INSIGHT, SHOULD GO THROUGH THE PROCESS OF BECOMING A BRAND. BECAUSE THIS JUST MEANS IT WOULD WIDEN ITS POWER IN THE WORLD AND OTHER PEOPLE CAN JOIN IN. THE WORLD IS IN GREAT NEED OF BETTER BRANDS. —ALAIN DE BOTTON

BRAND EVERYTHING

Brand thinking can be applied to advance people, places, organisations, movements, products, services and even materials or cultural concepts, to shape the way that people think and feel about them.

SOCIAL GOOD IS ALWAYS GOOD BRANDING. OR IS IT?

Before we dive into brand development, let's address a fundamental question. Is social good always good branding? These days, brands who put their social or environmental mission in the spotlight are taking the world by storm. But building your brand solely on your impact is not a guarantee for success, and it comes with risks that can take you by surprise. Consider these five points before you make social good the star of your show.

1 IF YOU CREATE A BRAND AROUND YOUR PHILANTHROPIC MODEL AND IT COMES UNDER FIRE, YOUR ENTIRE BUSINESS CAN SUFFER

American shoe manufacturer Tom's has built a business on the now much-replicated One-for-One model. In the past nine years Tom's has donated over 35 million shoes to children across the world, one for each pair sold through their commercial channels. The company has put One-for-One front and centre in all their branding and marketing efforts. To many consumers in the West, this is an easy-to-understand, warm-hearted initiative that they love to support and be associated with.

However, Tom's philanthropic model has recently come under fire. Critics point out that products donated to developing countries often distort the local markets, undercutting local suppliers and causing unemployment. The company now faces newspaper headlines directly linking them to the exact opposite of what they set out to achieve. When your social impact model comes under fire and is as intertwined with your brand as Tom's is with One-for-One, you are at risk of losing credibility and eventually sales.

2 WHAT YOU THINK IS A GREAT VALUE PROPOSITION MIGHT NOT BE OF GREAT VALUE TO YOUR AUDIENCE

In 2008 Indian mega conglomerate Tata launched its Nano, a 'car for the masses' priced at US$1,500, proclaiming their vision of an India where even the poorest can afford a car. The project failed to meet expectations, however, partially because no one was willing to buy what everyone saw as a car for poor people. By contrast, the Kenyan mobile payment system MPESA has an invaluable social impact because it provides people at all income levels with a money transfer service, effectively creating a bank for everyone.

THOUGH IT HAS ADVANCED THE LIFE OF MILLIONS, MPESA HAS NEVER PLAYED THIS UP

It is simply an effective, cheap and safe way to pay bills and receive payments. For MPESA, labelling their Kenyan customers 'poor' and offering them 'rescue' would make the brand less attractive than treating them like customers and providing a world-class service.

Similarly, the people behind the Dutch Weed Burger, a seaweed-based vegan hamburger, are former animal rights activists on a mission to get as many meat eaters to enjoy vegetarian and vegan food. But instead of highlighting the environmental benefits or cruelty-free aspects of their production method,

The Dutch Weed Burger is on a mission to convince meat eaters that going vegan is delicious.

they talk about its great taste. Staunch meat eaters aren't going to embrace vegan products unless they taste great, and environmental impact is just by-catch for them. In short: know your audience before you put your social impact in the spotlight. Your good intentions might disqualify you from the start.

3 THE IMPACT YOU ARE WORKING FOR MIGHT BE HARDER TO ACHIEVE THAN YOU EXPECT

Dutch chocolate brand Tony's Chocolonely started off in 2005 as an ambitious, 100% slave-free chocolate bar. Over the next few years, it emerged that Tony's couldn't guarantee that the entire supply chain of their chocolate was slave-free (nor could any other company in the industry). The original label on the chocolate bar wrapper featured a pictogram of a breaking chain, with the words '100% slave-free'. Today, it reads 'working together to become slave-free'. The brand has chosen to be open about the problems it is facing in the global chocolate trade and even shares critical articles on its Facebook page. Despite these setbacks, the popularity of the brand has not suffered; today it is a major competitor to the biggest chocolate brands on the shelves in the Netherlands. But it is safe to assume Tony's is the exception to the rule.

4 A BRAND BASED ON GOODWILL CAN FORGET TO COMPETE ON QUALITY

Branding something as socially or environmentally good might end up distracting you from delivering the best product or service that you can deliver. When you sell a feel-good product or service to an audience, that feel-good effect will not be enough to keep them coming back if the product is sub-par. This sounds obvious, but many organisations depend on their good intentions to keep them afloat. For example: you need a mobile phone charger to use on the road. You search the web for options and decide on a solar powered charger that is a little bit more expensive but environmentally friendly, plus for each sale the company delivers a matching device to someone in an electricity-poor environment. But after countless hours in the sun, it fails to charge your phone more than 20%.
The product fails to deliver what you paid for, and the feel-good effect evaporates. You bought from this company once, but will you ever buy anything else from them?

5 SOCIAL AND SUSTAINABLE WON'T BE DIFFERENTIATING FOREVER

Social and environmental impact will not always be the differentiating factors that they are at present. Today, when big banks are being rocked by scandals, the local 'green is good' bank stands out. When supermarket shelves are stocked with mass-produced foods, organic, handmade products stand out. But the day is coming (we hope) when every company's business model will be built around social and environmental responsibility, so in the long term, relying solely on this aspect as your advantage over others is a risky strategy. Consider a multi-value approach. What are your other differentiating qualities? When you deliver micro credit to the base of the pyramid, are you the best at service, or do you offer the lowest rates? Are you also offering free personal finance classes? Put that differentiation in the spotlight next to your social and environmental impact. Make sure you are recognised for what makes you different from the rest, the one thing that defines you, your delivery method or your amazing staff. Or add an emotional benefit besides a functional and an environmental one, like the sanitary product brand Yoni, which taps into a contemporary, sexy, confident-woman vibe.

Putting your social or environmental impact at the heart of your brand is often a first instinctual move when developing products or services designed to create change. But building the social into your brand is not a failsafe strategy. Consider your audience, your market and your positioning before you build your brand. If your goal is to create real impact, you might achieve that sooner through playing it down.

TONY'S CHOCOLONELY
Read about Tony's, the problems they have had in achieving their mission and how they handled this challenge on page 41.

CHAPTER 2
CASE STUDIES OF CHANGEMAKING BRANDS

CASE: YONI
RETHINKING PERIODS

How two women on a mission to revolutionise the femcare industry are attracting the attention of women and men.

TAGGED: RETAIL - PRODUCT - ORGANIC - WOMEN - B2C

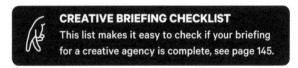
CREATIVE BRIEFING CHECKLIST
This list makes it easy to check if your briefing for a creative agency is complete, see page 145.

Organic sanitary products had been on the market for women for a decade, but the message of organic cotton tampons and pads had not reached women beyond a few die-hard organic shoppers. Yoni founders Mariah Mansvelt Beck and Wendelien Hebly want all women to have the toxic-free option.

From the start there have been two things Yoni had to tackle: 'We need to spread the word and offer the choice,' Hebly explains. 'Looking at what was available at that time, we saw that existing brands on the market were keeping themselves very eco-niche in distribution but also in look and feel. We see consumers worldwide becoming more and more aware of what they eat, and what they put on their faces... Why can't hygiene products be part of this shift? Why not create an organic feminine hygiene brand that is sexy?' As a result, Yoni was born.

Yoni's concept has remained the same ever since its inception, but the packaging, the name and the look and feel have changed. Initially, the brand was called 'FIP Organic'. Wendelien: 'At first we tried to design it ourselves, but we figured out that we weren't designers. Then we found someone to execute our ideas, which also didn't result in what we wanted. So we took one of the hardest decisions, which was to really clear the table of everything we'd been working on for a year and a half and start again.' The shift in positioning from 'FIP Organic' to 'Yoni, rethinking periods', was a major change. 'We were introduced to a small agency in the Netherlands, put our idea on the table, and conceived Yoni together.' Once the new name was set, the design of the brand was completed in three weeks. The resulting visual identity and packaging tells the story of Yoni through design. The packaging is simple and clean; what is on the box is what is in the box, and the capital 'Y' serves as a fun, witty nod to the crotch.

Yoni strikes a delicate balance between its minimalist image, a voice that demands to be heard and a witty sense of humour. The name Yoni is a bold choice, a word that means 'origin of life' as well as 'vagina' in Sanskrit. Not many people outside of India would know this; to them 'Yoni' sounds like a girl's name: personable and friendly. Yoni, the brand, immediately developed its own personality and tone of voice.

Yoni focuses its communication on spreading the story to a larger audience by being bold and creative. For a crowdfunding campaign, Mansvelt Beck and Hebly chose the slogan 'Chemicals are not for pussies'. Although their slogan is acceptable in Holland, a country known for its liberal culture, it might be offensive elsewhere, so it is not included on the packaging, which says simply: 'rethinking periods'.

WHY NOT CREATE AN ORGANIC FEMININE HYGIENE BRAND THAT IS SEXY?

The brand combines a missionary zeal with a sense of righteous indignation, all wrapped up in a soft, simple, approachable design. Wendelien: 'We never push people. We believe in both storytelling and making it easy for others to share this story and help spread the news so that people at least have the choice'. Their pitches are so clear and engaging that they draw interest from a wide audience, from investors to teenage girls.
The founders leave nothing to chance. 'We practise very hard, especially for the shorter pitches. Once you've invested a lot of time in getting your pitch as short as possible, then it's easier to talk about it for a longer period of time. Focus on that small one and then practise, practise, practise. All the feedback we got made us better.'

Yoni focused on free publicity, as opposed to paid advertising. Every bit of PR has come from speaking and promotion at events, social media, Kickstarter, videos and blogging. 'We would love to do something offline but online has a more targeted reach and we are able to see what comes out of the investment.' The Yoni team tries things out on a small scale to see what works and then makes it as strong as possible.

For instance at first they addressed women, but then realised that every man has at least one woman in his life, whether it's his wife or girlfriend or sister or a daughter whom he loves and wants to tell the story to. At events, Yoni stood at bathrooms to talk to women about the product, then learned posters could do the talking for them so they could be in more locations at once. 'Our concept is always the same but the story is evolving, and we continue to make it stronger. We try to find new ways of telling it.' Now that Yoni is sold in one of the biggest drugstore chains in the Netherlands, they are just starting their first experiment with paid advertisements.

People love Yoni so much, they come to the brand with suggestions of their own. 'There are so many women that email us and say, "Please, what can I do to spread the word?" It's a bit like a Tupperware Party.' Inspired by their fans, Yoni is currently building an ambassadors programme.

As a neuroscientist with a career working for big international companies, Hebly believes branding is crucial to the success of a social enterprise. 'I learned that it's not just about what story you tell, but also about the way you tell it. When you give a presentation, what people remember is 25% what you're saying and 75% how you tell it, how you look, how you stand, how you speak. That's how human beings are.'

RESULTS
Yoni is now available through one of the biggest drugstore chains in the Netherlands and is quickly amassing a tribe of voluntary brand ambassadors who help spread the word.

A great story is the biggest asset you have. When your story, your name and world-class design come together, you have a foundation for greatness.

More on Yoni
yoni.care
@Yonicare

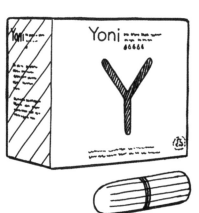
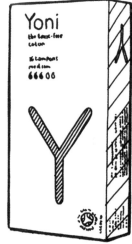

CASES: SUPERBETTER
HEADSPACE & THE SCHOOL OF LIFE
MIND GAMES

How three brands help us live a better life, from an American game designer tackling depression, to a British monk teaching meditation to Wall Street bankers, to a Swiss philosopher helping us make sense of ourselves, our work and our world.

TAGGED: PHILOSOPHY - MENTAL HEALTH - PERSONAL DEVELOPMENT - EDUCATION - APPS - B2C - B2B

Depression, stress, anxiety and mental disorders have long been delicate subjects, but as taboos about mental health are slowly being cast off, three companies have emerged that help us live better lives by offering joyful, playful and practical services. The diversity of their goals and methods demonstrates that the branding of mental health initiatives can be as varied and distinctive as their products and services.

1 THE BRANDING CASE OF SUPERBETTER

In 2009, game designer Jane McGonigal suffered a severe concussion that caused her to experience depression and even suicidal tendencies. To fight her way back to health, she did what she does best: she designed a game for herself. In it, players set a goal (health or wellness) and invite others to play with them and keep them on track. She called it 'Jane: the Concussion Slayer' and put it online, and to her surprise, people started playing it. Realising that she could address conditions beyond concussions and that there could be a wider audience for the game, she rebranded it 'SuperBetter', verbalising her goal to not just get back to health, but to get even healthier than before, and the rest is gaming history.

Over 500,000 people have played the game since its launch. Today, SuperBetter is an everyday digital coach that increases players' mental resilience to help them achieve goals and tackle challenges. The SuperBetter brand is relentlessly optimistic, with a bubblegum rainbow look and feel.
The language is playful and borrows from a childlike world of quests: allies, power-ups, bad guys and future boosts abound. The brand has now expanded to include a book and a social enterprise.

2 THE BRANDING CASE OF HEADSPACE

Headspace is an app with a single voice guiding you through daily meditation sessions. That voice belongs to a former Buddhist monk, the app's co-founder Andy Puddicombe. Though initially sceptical of online meditation, Puddicombe warmed to the idea of developing an app because he saw its potential to bring meditation to large audiences. He had already used meditation as a way to reduce stress for patients with insomnia and high blood pressure while working at a medical clinic. The financial crisis of the early 2000s brought a stream of bankers into his office, and he realised that he had to bring meditation to them in a very different way in order for them to accept it as a treatment. Puddicombe translated Sanskrit terms into English, toned down the esoteric vocabulary and shortened the sessions. The method took off. One of Puddicombe's patients became his business partner and the app was born.

Today, Headspace calls itself 'a gym membership for the mind'. It markets itself primarily to 'blokes', guys who have little interest in spirituality or Eastern philosophies. Headspace brings in a scientific angle, quoting research into the effects of meditation. The app has a slick interface softened by pastel colours and an attractive illustration style reminiscent of Google. Sanskrit terms and temple bells are both conspicuously absent. The first words you hear are: 'Hi, my name is Andy', spoken in a very British accent. It is no surprise that the Silicon Valley tech set has embraced it fully. At the intersection of self-help and business, mindfulness is now thriving.

3 THE BRANDING CASE: THE SCHOOL OF LIFE

Founded by philosopher Alain de Botton in 2008, The School of Life is an extension of his personal brand of 'everyday philosophy', helping people learn how to live wisely and well, addressing the big life questions that all of us ask about our loves, careers and relationships. It is a one-stop shop for emotional intelligence, offering classes, therapy, books, videos and events. The defining factor of its success is the positive frame it has created. 'We are in the business of giving people good ideas about improving their quality of life, from coping with anxiety to managing relationships to getting a better handle on their work. It's the thing I'm proudest to have done in my life.

WE HAVE CREATED A BRAND IN AN AREA THAT USED TO BE TOTALLY UNBRANDED

The brand exudes comfort, wisdom and optimism. A contemporary, chic graphic identity gives the school a clear, sunny face. Its voice is wise but down-to-earth, generous and kind, always ready to question itself and to offer up a dose of wit without making light of tough topics. In the digital sphere, its YouTube channel offers short videos on a range of topics visualised and made relatable by illustration, collage and animation. The brand's focus, however, is very consciously on physical experiences. Their classrooms and therapy spaces are a cross between a Scandinavian design hotel and a hipster café. Their books and tools are designed with a gorgeous simplicity on special materials rich with textures and sometimes even scents. It is clear that a life well lived, according to this school, is also a life filled with beauty.

RESULTS

SuperBetter has been played by over 500,000 people and Headspace has been downloaded more than eleven million times. Only nine years after its founding, The School of Life now has ten stores in twelve cities around the world, creating an entirely new market for personal development and therapy services.

Even initiatives concerning topics as taboo as depression, illness, anxiety and stress can be turned into brands that people embrace and love to be seen with. The branding of mental health is as much a mind game as the philosophies the brands represent.

More on SuperBetter
superbetter.com
@SuperBetter

More on The School of Life
theschooloflife.com
@TheSchoolOfLife

More on Headspace
headspace.com
@Get_Headspace

CASE: BRCK
RUGGED INTERNET FOR PEOPLE AND THINGS

How a tech company from Nairobi is catching the world's attention purely on the potential of its product.

TAGGED: TECH · CONNECTIVITY · B2B · B2C

The way we work is changing, and the way we educate our children is changing, moving more and more online, even for people who live in places where electricity and Internet connections are problematic. Lack of access to electricity and connectivity is widening the already massive gap in knowledge and economic opportunities for people in low income countries. With BRCK, a portable, self-powered Wi-Fi hotspot designed and engineered in Kenya, information can flow freely, the way it is intended.

BRCK founders David Kobia, Juliana Rotich, and Erik Hersman know first-hand how crucial it is to have access to the Internet. As the catalysts of enterprises like iHub and Ushahidi, they rose to global fame by building software to map out reports of violence during the 2008 elections in Kenya. With regular power outages comes modem downtime, with remote locations comes little or no signal. What if you had a self-powered Wi-Fi device that was built for rugged environments like the African countryside or city? What if you could connect a classroom in remote Turkana to great online educational content?

When the idea for BRCK was born, its founders' renown and respect in the tech scene galvanised the support of thousands worldwide. The story of a product that met the needs of millions of people around the world, that was designed in Africa and for Africa, was a siren call, expertly told by Juliana Rotich through platforms like TED and global media.

After securing funding, the trio quickly enlisted Kenya's best talents to join their ranks. Among the first hires was designer Jeff Maina, now the creative director and guardian of the BRCK brand. He works closely with the founders to create a holistic brand that does justice to the promise of the product.

Jeff: 'Anything that goes out into the world goes through my team. I now have a designer and front end developer to make sure that everything we do exudes quality. From the product to the package, from opening the box to logging in to the dashboard or the cloud, it should all look great and provide a perfect user experience. We are building a world-class product for emerging economies.'

JUST BECAUSE WE DON'T HAVE A MILLION DOLLARS DOESN'T MEAN IT SHOULD LOOK SUBSTANDARD

The BRCK brand is as rugged, reliable and down-to-earth as its product, both visually and verbally. Bold blacks and bright yellows combine with a clean graphic language that can compare to that of the best tech brands in the world. The visual appearance of the brand contrasts with the mud and dust in the documentary videos of the BRCK team on expedition to some of the remotest parts of Kenya. Maina: 'We go on expeditions to test the product, and we film this process. And people are impressed. We've always worked with stories. We tell what the product can do for you. The story sells.'

BRCK is quickly expanding its line, and a brand portfolio is emerging. It chose to create sub-brands for different products to ensure that different brand audiences don't get lost in a mass of products not intended for their eyes. One such sub-brand is the Kio Kit, a set of tablets bundled with top educational content, designed to help schools make full use of the BRCK's potential to bring world-class education to underserved rural and urban schools. Because BRCK is growing fast both as a

product and as a team, they are now really locking down the guidelines for the brand in order for the brand portfolio to continue to develop while remaining consistent and true to the unique set of beliefs that drives the BRCK movement.

Having an in-house creative team completely embedded in the company culture and values is an asset to the company that is more than worth the investment involved. BRCK has become an inspiration for both the region and the continent. Maina: 'All the countries in the region are looking at us and seeing what is possible. We are setting a benchmark.'

RESULTS
Since its start in 2013 BRCK has seen growth without relying on traditional marketing or advertising methods. To date they have sold 2,600 units.

An in-house creative director is key to building and protecting a brand. Maintaining quality in every aspect lays the foundation for a great return on investment. When meaning is built into a product, your brand thrives on storytelling.

More on BRCK
brck.com
@brcknet

CASE: MAKEY MAKEY
THINK ABOUT THE BOX

How a product inspired by the maker movement was repackaged to reach its full potential.

TAGGED: CHILDREN - TECH - CREATIVITY - B2C

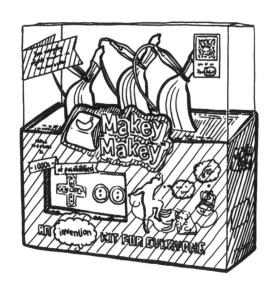

Makey Makey is the brainchild of Jay Silver and Eric Rosenbaum, who believe that everyone is creative, inventive, and imaginative, and that technology can be presented in a way that enables people of all ages to play and experiment with it. Based on this insight they developed Makey Makey, a simple invention kit for beginners and experts doing art, engineering, and everything in between. The first commercial edition of Makey Makey was realised through the support of 11,000 backers on Kickstarter.

'After the first Kickstarter, we knew we'd need to ship our product in something,' Silver explains, 'but we were completely focused on the product and user experience. The packaging was a last minute thing. We went with the simplest type of box, and I happened to live next door to a design wizard who said, "I can design you a box in a couple days." Boom, instant box. And so it was for a few years.'

Makey Makey started as a niche product for the maker movement and was initially only sold by the inventors online in a small, green e-commerce box featuring the circuit board and a number of things it could connect to. Fairly soon, however, the retail world came knocking, and Makey Makey realised that a chain like Toys"R"Us could help them reach a far larger audience. But to be able to sell at scale, they needed to upgrade their packaging. The simple box designed for the kickstarted campaign just could not compete with the visual assault in the toy aisles.

Following a personal intuition, Silver and the team decided to work with the Chicago-based agency Merge to create a design that would fit the unconventional nature of the kit. 'Makey Makey as an "object" really isn't all that interesting; what matters is the creative behaviour that it enables as a tool. It's the world reconsidered. The new packaging needed to vivify this ... easy, right?(!)' Makey Makey's signature red features prominently on the new boxes, which boldly display the kit's alligator clips attached to banana cut-outs, fun and creative elements that illustrate the product's purpose and proposition.

RESULTS

Makey Makey is now sold at stores like such as Walmart, Best Buy and Barnes & Noble, as well as on platforms like Amazon, and of course through the inventors' website. Over 400,000 units have been sold, bringing the maker movement to the grand stage.

In order to grow your movement and realise your vision, designing for a commercial context is necessary to achieve scale.

More on Makey Makey
makeymakey.com
@thejoylabz

USING THE OCEAN WITHOUT USING IT UP

In a time when climate change is accelerating, oceans are becoming plastic soup, coral reefs are dying and few people seem to be doing anything about it, you would not expect a marine biologist to thrive. And yet Dr Ayana Elizabeth Johnson repeatedly manages to catch the attention of policymakers, citizens and fellow scientists, and convince them action is needed.

TAGGED: CONSERVATION - MOVEMENTS - ACTIVISM - PERSONAL BRANDING

What do all good leaders have in common? They stand for something. They make sure the right people know about it, and they make a plan to attract their support. Great leaders think a lot like brand strategists. Dr Ayana Elizabeth Johnson is thoughtful and deliberate about building her profile, crafting compelling proposals for action and spreading them far and wide through platforms like National Geographic and The New York Times, all in the service of the ocean and the communities that depend on it.

In her quest to influence government and corporate policy, scientific discussion and consumer behaviour, Dr Johnson's ammunition is ideas. In a sector where spoof awards are handed out for the most impenetrable academic writing, Dr Johnson stands out for the clarity with which she communicates.

Her clarity is in part the result of her community approach to conservation. 'I spend a lot of time interviewing people in coastal communities, talking to them on the street or on the docks.

WHEN YOU SEE THEIR EYES GLAZE OVER, OR IF THEY LOOK CONFUSED ... THAT'S ALL THE FEEDBACK YOU NEED

The basic principles of ocean conservation are simple. If you can't explain them simply, then you need to work on explaining them better. If we catch fewer fish and we leave more in the ocean to make babies, there will be more fish. There are parts of conservation that are really that simple.' Unfortunately what resonates with one person doesn't necessarily resonate with all. 'It is a process of iterating on word choice until it is perfectly clear, not just to one person but to many people.'

Her writing also contributes to her use of clear language. To date, Dr Johnson has published over 50 essays on her work and thinking on National Geographic.

THERE IS NOTHING LIKE WRITING TO HELP ME UNDERSTAND WHAT I THINK AND HOW I CAN BEST EXPRESS IT

Pursuing clarity requires a big time investment. Dr Johnson: 'It takes so much work to distil things to the point where you are really clear, but it is always worth the effort. For example, the phrase "using the ocean without using it up" is something that took me about a year to formulate while working on an ocean zoning project. There are certainly plenty of real reasons why people would disagree with your approach, but I don't want to have disagreements because of a misunderstanding. I don't want to get caught up in situations where you are speaking past each other and you can't get anything done.'

Dr Johnson has learned to look at the human incentives at play too. 'This low-tech and low-cost fish trap design I created, which reduces bycatch by 80%, would never have gained traction if I hadn't also proved to the government that using it would not hurt fishermen's incomes. Because the biggest factor in policy change is political will, and fishermen are voters. To build political will we need to understand where people are coming from.'

Dr Johnson avoids using words that will alienate people. Sustainability has become a buzzword with a lot of baggage and people aren't really sure what it means, but no one has any trouble getting behind 'Using the ocean without using it up'.

Doing what is right for the economy and what is right for the environment are often seen as incompatible. Dr Johnson: 'When you talk about conservation, people think you want to go and save dolphins. And dolphins are fine but that is absolutely not why I do ocean conservation. People thought I was the ocean equivalent of a tree hugger, that I cared more about sea creatures than I did about people.' That misperception can result in not getting your ideas implemented.

Once she made it clear that to her, ocean conservation is about people, not fish, it opened a lot of doors to new conversations. 'I am not just an environmentalist; I am an advocate for these communities. I am someone who cares about public health and safety and economy and traditions that are all tied to a healthy ocean.'

As a former TED resident, Dr Johnson recognises the power of stories in pushing for conservation. 'It's not my own story that is terribly useful or unique. Instead, I spend a lot of time listening to and reading about other people's experiences with the ocean. Older fishermen telling me about what it used to be like and how they wished it would be like that again. People telling me how hard it is to make a living now. If children have to leave their coastal community to get jobs, that is breaking up families. It's really dangerous to people's cultures when you lose the resources that your culture was built on. I feel very lucky that people share their stories with me, so I can show other people why all this stuff matters, why we have to fix overfishing and climate change and pollution: because people's lives and jobs and cultures are at stake.'

The urgency many conservationists feel, to 'wake people up' to the dangerous predicament we are in, often results in negative messaging that can push people away. 'There is a really fine balance between optimism and doom. I worry about people painting too rosy a picture of the state of our planet. I don't want to pretend that everything is fine.'

I AM HAPPY TO DESCRIBE IN DETAIL JUST HOW MUCH OF A MESS WE HAVE MADE, AS HUMANS, LIVING ON PLANET EARTH. BUT AT THE SAME TIME, IF YOU END THERE, YOU'VE ACHIEVED NOTHING

'You've made people scared, worried and often they ignore it because what can they do? It's a delicate balance of saying, yes we have a really big problem on our hands, but here are some real solutions that we should all be implementing ourselves individually and that we should be pushing for as policy changes and changes to corporate practices.'

There is a somewhat loosely coordinated hashtag for solutions in ocean conservation on social media: #oceanoptimism, which Dr Johnson uses often. 'Not to say everything is fine, but to talk about what is working and do more of those things. We need to build on each other's successes and amplify those stories across the world, so people are inspired, encouraged and can see the roadmap to being more and more effective.'

As a marine biologist, conservation strategist, adjunct professor at New York University, one of the leaders of the March for Science and founder of the new consulting firm Ocean Collectiv, Dr Johnson wears many different hats. Yet across all these roles, she has a singular focus. Her mission is to create, implement, and amplify the best ideas in conservation, so we can use the ocean without using it up. Being recognised for this mission is of crucial importance to Dr Johnson's impact. The decision makers in her field need to know who she is. When it comes down to who's leading the conservation organisations, hiring people or funding projects, it's not a big group of people, so reputation is crucial.

FOR A LOT OF OPPORTUNITIES IN LIFE THERE IS NO APPLICATION PROCESS

'People just ask around: who might be able to do this? It helps for people in your field to know who you are. Having a strong profile that is linked to my professional philosophy has been really helpful for me. People know where I stand, what kinds of things I think about, how I prioritise different conservation approaches. I'm really glad that I have the blog with National

Geographic because it's a record of my thoughts, a body of work that presents my views.' Dr Johnson can refer people to the work, and the work refers people to her.

Of course, we'd all love a blog on a popular website, but how do you get there? 'There is no real formula to it. A lot of it is serendipity, having a strong network of colleagues and collaborators.' That's not to say you don't have any control over it. 'You just have to put yourself out there and say: I am really interested in doing this, is there a way we can make it happen? And the answer is yes more often than I would have expected.'

Recently, the incoming requests are more in the area of public speaking and events, which have great network benefits.

I WOULD ENCOURAGE PEOPLE TO EXPAND THEIR NETWORKS IN WAYS THEY CAN'T IMMEDIATELY PREDICT THE VALUE OF

'Most of the events I go to are outside of my own field, and the people I collaborate with do not have the same background as me. I find that helps me understand how to reach new audiences and it helps me to be known in different circles – this is critical because ocean conservation (and most big challenges!) are inherently multi-disciplinary.'

RESULTS

At 37, Dr Johnson has an impressive list of successful conservation interventions on her CV. Her design of a fish trap with escape slots reduces bycatch by ~80%, without reducing fishermen's incomes, and it is now required by law in several countries. She led the Caribbean's first successful island-wide ocean zoning project, resulting in the protection of one-third of Barbuda's coastal waters. As a leader of the March for Science, she helped bring together over a million people worldwide to advocate for the role of science in policymaking.

In order to get people to implement your proposal for change, your ideas need to be clear and relevant to the audience. Carve them out over time, test them again and again. A strong profile positions you at the optimal place to take opportunities as you pursue and create them.

More on Dr Johnson
ayanaelizabeth.com
@ayanaeliza
oceancollectiv.co
@oceancollectiv

SHARE YOUR CHALLENGE

Are you struggling to find clarity in your own messaging? Share what you are working on with our community to get feedback and discuss ideas. Join our Facebook Group: facebook.com/groups/brandthechange

CASE: SANERGY/FRESH LIFE

BRANDING IS SILVER, CO-CREATION IS GOLD

How a line of pay-per-use toilets became the preferred option for residents in Nairobi's informal settlements*.

TAGGED: SUSTAINABLE ENERGY - B2C - BASE OF THE PYRAMID - SOCENT

* Heavily populated urban areas where housing units have been constructed on (illegally) occupied land, characterised by substandard housing and squalor. Popularly known as slums.

In low-income countries, lack of hygienic sanitation is a leading cause of disease, death and loss of GDP. Sanergy designs and manufactures low-cost, high-quality sanitation facilities and collects the waste, which it converts into products such as organic fertiliser and renewable energy. The sanitation units are run by a network of local residents who purchase and operate them.

On the one side, Sanergy has an international audience of investors, governments, journalists and socially aware citizens. Quite on the other side, it has its customers and operators, residents of underserved urban communities in Kenya. The two groups could not be more different, and when Sanergy discovered that neither its name nor its positioning resonated at ground level, it could not afford to turn a deaf ear, so it decided to give the units a separate brand.

'We thought we would choose a Swahili name,' says Medora Brown, manager of communications at Sanergy, 'but people really liked the English names we proposed. They felt having an English name implied that the brand was bigger than just informal settlements, bigger than Kenya. It had the sound of an international brand, and they liked that. What we also found is that consumers aren't really compelled by messaging that you should use hygienic sanitation so that you or your kids don't get sick. What really resonated was something aspirational and motivational: how to a build a better, more prosperous life.' As a result, Fresh Life was born.

The co-creation process is ingrained in everything Sanergy does. 'We use it in every aspect of our business, including the design development of the sanitation units themselves. We solicit feedback from the toilet operators, and we solicit feedback from the users.' Based on the feedback, Sanergy has adapted the squat plate design, installed hooks and mirrors, and is rolling out a design with squat supports for customers with impaired mobility. 'Since it is a pay-per-use service, you want customers to be as happy as possible with the experience and come back again and again.'

TESTING WITH THE COMMUNITY IS CRUCIAL

'To have our team sitting at a conference table and making decisions around what would appeal more to our target users does not make sense. Most of our team is Kenyan, and many are from the communities we serve, but soliciting feedback from our target users provides us with information we wouldn't otherwise have.'

When it comes to the visibility of brands in many African cities, the only limit is the size of a building's facade. Entire homes and office buildings are hand-painted in a brand's colours and splashed with logos. Three-storey billboards line the roads. In the informal settlements this is less true, and with their bright blue paint and yellow logo, the Fresh Life units stand out like beacons in the grey and brown streets. 'We found that the most effective method for achieving brand visibility was to brand the toilets themselves with big Fresh Life logos. It just became really hard to miss us. We are very present and that is intentional. On the door of each toilet it says "choo" (Swahili for "toilet") and the price, to make it very clear what we're selling.'

Demonstrating the permanence of Sanergy's presence in the settlements is crucial. To build brand awareness, Sanergy organises events under the Fresh Life flag. They use World Toilet Day and other related holidays to raise awareness about good sanitation measures, and even hold contests and football competitions. 'One thing we found is that working in these communities is a chicken and egg thing. We can't operate in these communities unless we have their trust, but they will not trust us until we operate well.' explains Medora. Accordingly, they have opened two offices in the area, each in key slums. 'We work a lot with village elders and area chiefs so that they're on board with our work and are advocating for us in the community.' Sanergy doesn't just convince them by talking about the effects of better hygiene. 'We create jobs in areas where unemployment is over 40%, and people take note. It means the entire community is healthier and more prosperous. And that is our goal in the end.'

SANERGY'S MARKETING CURRENTLY HAS TWO AIMS: TO INCREASE USAGE AND TO CONVERT NON-USERS

For a new campaign, developed with community input, they are focusing on clean, close, and cheap. 'Despite knowing our product by sight, not everyone knows what we offer; or they think we are out of their price range, despite the price being clearly marked on the side.' Based on extensive focus group work, Sanergy's marketing team has developed a campaign that emphasises these aspects of their services. One innovation for this campaign is to have the communications be in Swahili, as focus group participants said it was more compelling to see ads written 'in the way the people speak'. The team is also starting to use the term 'bei ya mtaa' or 'local price', as opposed to 'muzungu', the (often higher) foreigner price.

Such brand building and marketing is integral to Sanergy's business and social impact model. 'We are trying to get people who make less than two dollars a day to spend five cents of that on our toilets. It is absolutely crucial that they understand our value proposition. So whether you call that community education or outreach or marketing or branding, it is educating people on how they can keep themselves and their families healthy, which, in turn, improves the well-being of the community as a whole.'

> **◠◠ GOING TO MARKET**
> Read more about marketing to underserved communities in the guest essay by Grant Tudor on page 204.

RESULTS

The impact of Sanergy's efforts can be measured directly by weighing the human waste collected, and to date, Fresh Life has safely collected and removed 12,000 tons of human waste from informal urban settlements and created 900 jobs in the communities it serves. It is currently logging more than 55,000 users every day. With branding driving direct results in the increase in use, the local team of brand experts and marketeers is helping the company and the community to thrive.

When building a brand for a community whose life, motivations and considerations are far removed from your own, a co-creative process and continuous testing are vital to building trust in your brand and helping your venture thrive.

More on Sanergy
saner.gy
@Sanergy

CASE: TONY'S CHOCOLONELY
RAISING THE BAR

How a fictional chocolate brand became
the leader of the pack.

TAGGED: FOOD · FAIRTRADE · HUMAN RIGHTS · RETAIL · B2C

**The last person on earth who could have foreseen the
success of anti-slavery chocolate brand Tony's Chocolonely
was its creator, Dutch journalist Teun (Tony) van de Keuken.
In 2003, as part of an ongoing TV series exposing the ills and
oddities of the food industry, van de Keuken exposed
a world of slavery behind the chocolate bar. Investigating
whether it was at all possible to produce chocolate untainted
by slave labour, he created a fictional product purely for
investigative purposes. His prototype bar resonated with the
Dutch public, and the brand is now celebrating its twelfth
year.**

When Dutch designer Arjen Klinkenberg, known as Klink,
offered to create a wrapper for van de Keuken's prototype
slave-free milk chocolate bar, neither was aware of the raging
success they were about to unleash. In a little over ten minutes,
Klink created a bold, eye-popping label that could have come
straight out of *Charlie and the Chocolate Factory*. He also
flaunted convention by making it red, a colour normally
reserved for dark chocolate. Klink: 'It was my point to do it
differently from the other chocolate brands. So I chose the
colour red instead of blue to reflect the alarming message, but
above all to make people think about what they pick from the
chocolate rack. Especially in the first years we often got
complaints from people, but our message was: think, read the
packaging, be aware of your actions.'

The first batch of bars sold out rapidly, and an incredibly
popular (and lucrative) chocolate brand was born. The first,
simple milk chocolate bar has grown into an entire line of
products ranging from special-edition liquorice chocolate bars
to chocolate milk. Van de Keuken, whose heart was in
investigative journalism, not in running a business, handed over

the reins to a business team, while Klink is now the full time creative guru, guiding the development of brand experiences for the Tony's team.

Both the company and the brand have grown exponentially, but Klink and van de Keuken's moxie is still at the heart of it all. 'It's set in our core values: outspoken, entrepreneurial, wilful and having fun along the way.' The company's vision, mission and values are not just words on a page. For example, their progress towards their goals is discussed critically every two weeks with the supply chain team. Every quarter, they dive into their values and how they are bringing them to life across everything they do. Twice a year the team goes to Chocademy to dive deeper into their own motivations and development and deepen the core values.

Crafting an ethical, fun and outspoken company culture is clearly not left to chance. And that culture needs input from the outside world as well. 'We challenge ourselves by inviting inspirational guest speakers for breakfast sessions, and Teun keeps us on our toes, as do our friends.' The first group of Tony's friends, socially engaged individuals, has grown with the brand throughout the years. 'People wear our shirts, do their school presentations about Tony's, make art out of the wrappers, or wallpaper their homes with them. We call them our Serious Friends.'

Klink sums up the acts of love with clear joy: 'One morning I arrived at the office and there were lipstick kisses all across our windows. It's just incredible.' What inspires these acts of love from Tony's friends? 'I think people love the degree of attention to things and the way we speak.' The friends are crucial to the Tony's brand.

THE WORD "FRIEND" ALREADY SHOWS IT IS A TWO-WAY STREET: WE INVITE THEM TO OUR BIRTHDAY PARTIES, WE ANSWER THEIR SOCIAL MEDIA POSTS

Though many brands throw around the word 'community', 'friends' and 'engagement', few really build actual human relationships. For ten years Tony's has been at the forefront of building communities, and social media has always been a big part of that strategy, way before other brands clued up on what value a community holds.

'Our mission is based on working together, so social media is the logical approach. We put a lot of time into conversing on Facebook, but also inviting people to stop by our office and showering them with chocolate.' The presentation of the annual report is a public event that friends are invited to and anyone can sign up for. It is part forum for discussion with guests and part party, and it is streamed online. Another example of creating a two-way friendship is their monthly meetup on a Friday afternoon about a new product or recipe, with, of course, chocolate and beer. Anyone can join and critical questions are encouraged. The bar for getting in touch with the team is set purposefully low. Tony's only self-owned shop, Tony's Thuis (Tony's Home), is connected to the headquarters in Amsterdam. Furnished like a living room, you can step in for chocolate and a chat with one of the team members. 'Our friends are the most important thing. Alone we can make slave-free chocolate; together we can make all chocolate 100% slave-free. So we ask people to join in and show them that we don't just want them eating our chocolate, but to understand and share our story as well.'

Tony's makes it easy for its fans and friends to spread the word. People can sign up to be a 'serious friend' and to help spread the story, sign petitions and support events. For younger friends who want to give a presentation at their school about Fairtrade chocolate, there is a special kit available to download for free, with a presentation template, a video, goodies and more.

Tony's has been truly embraced by the public at large, not an easy feat for a chocolate with a strong ethical message. Today everything the brand does exudes a happy counterculture vibe. 'It is our goal to show the chocolate giants you can be commercially successful without exploiting people. You can preach doom and gloom, but that won't make your chocolate sell faster. We like to look at the bright side and believe that being a little too naive is better than being a little too negative. We love what we do, keep laughing, and are full of energy to move chocolate mountains.'

Despite over a decade of hard work, Tony's is still not able to guarantee a 100% slave-free bar, nor are any of its competitors. The brand doesn't shun the debate, and even placed a critical article by van de Keuken on its Facebook page. Value Chain Director and man on the ground in Africa, Arjen Boekhold: 'Back in 2005, even our certified Fairtrade supplier had to admit he was not able to guarantee slave-free beans. In 2013, our beans became 100% traceable.' In the past two years, the cacao butter (50% of the chocolate) has also become fully traceable for all their bars. By 2018 Tony's expects to be truly 100% slave-free.

In 2005, the label on the front of the wrapper, underneath a pictogram of a breaking chain, read '100% slave-free'. Today, it's 'Together we make chocolate 100% slave-free'. The complexity of the issue is not easily explained. 'We spread the story out into segments and share it on social media, with our website as an archive with more background. We've also had a film made (*The Chocolate Case*) that explains the struggle. We're not afraid of failing as long as we learn from it and share our failures and lessons with everyone. We believe people should be able to trust a brand with a social mission and therefore it's our duty to be as transparent as we can be.'

RESULTS

Tony's Chocolonely has gone from investigative journalism project to second-largest chocolate brand in the Netherlands and is expanding across Europe and the US.

Clash with your environment: the bland can't lead the bland. When faced with setbacks in your impact model, be as open and transparent about it as possible.

More on Tony's Chocolonely
tonyschocolonely.com
@TonyChocolonely

NO ONE SHOULD FACE CANCER ALONE

How a hundred-year-old organisation reinvented its brand to double its impact and increase its fundraising by tens of millions of pounds.

TAGGED: HEALTH - FUND RAISING - COMMUNITY - NOT-FOR-PROFIT

For over a hundred years Macmillan (under various names and with various faces) has supported people living with cancer. From the moment patients are diagnosed, through their treatment and beyond, Macmillan offers services ranging from help with financial worries to information about treatment, to advice about work, even a listening ear when you feel lonely.

In the early 2000s, Macmillan was facing some significant challenges. The organisation was increasingly being seen as old-fashioned and irrelevant. Though cancer rates were rising sharply, people were living longer with the disease and consequently their needs were changing. For many people Macmillan was associated exclusively with end-of-life care (their nurses were popularly known as 'angels of death'), a misperception that kept people from turning to the organisation for support from the moment they were diagnosed. Despite being in the top ten for fundraising performance among UK charities, Macmillan ranked only 28th in awareness.

With over two million people living with cancer in the UK, Macmillan refused to sit back and watch this decline. 'It became really clear that incremental changes were not going to help us. We really needed to focus on building our brand and doing things significantly differently,' says Ali Sanders, Head of Brand and Creative at Macmillan. The charity looked to a new brand strategy, positioning, name, verbal identity and visual identity to turn the tide.

It was, however, easier said than done. 'Back in 2003, there was really poor awareness of brand within the organisation and we weren't working with the right agencies to address such fundamental challenges. After some trial and error, we got in touch with the Advertising Agencies Register and they helped us to set up the process and create a really robust brief for a tender,' Sanders explains. Gaining support within the organisation was a whole other challenge, and Sanders believes that in general, the not-for-profit sector has been slower to embrace the role of branding than the commercial sector has. 'There is this perception that it is about logos, visual identities and communications. "Why would you invest in branding when you can put it into services?" That was the kind of thinking we were up against.' A visionary director, Judy Beard, led the effort and involved the Board of Trustees in thinking about the kind of organisation they wanted to be, giving senior staff ownership of the process. London-based agency Wolff Olins was selected for the work in 2004, and after an 18-month process the rebrand was launched with great success.

At the heart of the transformation was the brand idea, 'life force', which drives both services and communications. While other cancer charities are focused on either finding a cure (Cancer Research UK) or caring for the terminally ill (Marie Curie), Macmillan has firmly positioned itself in the area of 'living with cancer'. They changed their name from 'Macmillan Cancer Relief' to 'Macmillan Cancer Support', a positive, everyday source of help for anyone affected by the disease.

The new brand identity also needed to feel approachable and inclusive rather than institutional and authoritative if Macmillan hoped to grow its volunteer base and its ability to support more people. To drive a movement that everyone could be a part of, Wolff Olins developed a radical visual identity with a unique, handcrafted font and bold silhouettes in a palette of bright greens. The brand expression is not only memorable and distinctive, but also compassionate, inspiring and action-driven, evincing a deep understanding of the strange new world that people can find themselves in after a cancer diagnosis.

WE NEEDED TO CREATE A MOVEMENT IN ORDER TO REACH THE NUMBERS OF PEOPLE WITH CANCER WHO NEED SUPPORT

Placed among the logos developed by other charities competing for the same fundraising pounds, Macmillan's bold green look stands out. 'The identity has been very successful in helping us to stand out and be recognised. Over the years, we've also developed and refined it to improve the way it works with our diverse range of audiences.'

'We've also done quite fundamental pieces of work over the years to explore different aspects of the brand beyond the identity, for instance, around engaging more volunteers. A whole new way of thinking came out of that brand work.' An expression of this thinking is Macmillan's website, The Source, source.macmillan.org.uk, where people can share their own practical tips on showing support to people

THE REPUTATION TURNAROUND
Stuck with the wrong reputation? Go to page 196.

living with cancer. The Macmillan movement is intensely human. Their Coffee Mornings help people gather over coffee and donate the cost of their cuppa to Macmillan in the process. Nights In are intimate fundraising events people can organise with their friends. Macmillan shares comfort food recipes and music playlists to make them fun, relaxed evenings. An online community has been set up to enable people to share their questions about cancer and offer their own experiences, knowledge and support. The community is thriving. 'This was a very big step for the organisation.

The thinking was, aren't we the experts?' But opening up the brand to truly involve everyone has been crucial in attracting new audiences and growing their services.

Today Macmillan is a far more self-assured organisation with a clear idea of its role. As Sanders says, 'We define branding as how people think and feel about us,' which makes everyone inside the organisation a brand ambassador. She sees her role at Macmillan as building relationships and influencing the entire team. 'Everyone is responsible for the experience that we offer, and therefore they are directly influencing how people think and feel about us. The brand is now completely embedded in everything we do.'

Sanders has deliberately kept the brand team small. 'We're here to guide people, we're here to influence, we're here to make sure that they are equipped with what they need. It's about everybody going out and living the brand.' The online brand portal, be.macmillan.org, is part of that philosophy, helping people build consistent yet living brand expressions and offering brand identity guidelines, booklets and reports. New employees of Macmillan go through brand training to ensure they understand the brand. Ongoing research into clients and their context is constantly unearthing new insights. Sanders: 'People often see branding as something that has a beginning and an end. In most organisations there's a brand project and when it is considered done they move on to other things. Because we fundamentally positioned brand as how people think and feel about us, it's never done, it's constantly evolving.'

RESULTS

After a £120,000 rebrand, Macmillan has a strong position amongst charities. It now ranks joint fourth in spontaneous brand awareness, income has increased from £97.7m in 2005 to £244.9m in 2016, and most importantly, in 2016 the charity gave 1.4 million people personal support, either face-to-face or over the phone, and helped millions more through their information and support materials. The new brand has also helped attract better talent to the organisation. One in two people interviewing for a job at Macmillan cite the brand as the reason they want to work there. More volunteers have joined, and strategic partnerships, for example with Boots pharmacy, have provided Macmillan with a high street presence.

A clear understanding of your image and the changing times and context you operate in is vital to survival. Taking a clear position, standing out from the crowd and creating inclusive and outstanding experiences are all crucial to building a movement.

More on Macmillan Cancer Support
macmillan.org.uk
@macmillancancer

CASE: THNK
THE NEW SCHOOL

How an Amsterdam school went from zero to one and is defining a new category in education.

TAGGED: INNOVATION - HIGHER EDUCATION - B2B

THNK, the School of Creative Leadership, offers Executive Leadership programmes and in-company programmes at its hubs in Amsterdam, Vancouver and Lisbon.

While a 'b-school' teaches students about business, and a 'd-school' teaches design, THNK is a 'c-school'. Menno van Dijk, co-founder: 'We positioned THNK between the b-school and the d-school, an alphabetic positioning. We are not a blend, we are defining a new category.' Defining a new category is a tough branding challenge, but van Dijk sees only advantages. 'It is easier than defining it as a superior concept within an existing category. You could only do that by having higher quality or lower cost. Particularly in the area of executive education, you are up against some serious names.

IF YOU DEFINE YOURSELF AS A COMPLETELY NEW CATEGORY, YOU PUT YOUR COMPETITION AT A DISTANCE

If the competition then turns around and says "We do that too", they are compromising their own brand positioning and it sounds less credible because they are so strong in their own field.'

The THNK brand had to deliver credibility fast, because its programmes are not cheap. 'I did my most cost-efficient cost breakdown and divided that by the number of people I was expecting to attract. That defined a minimum price. Then we looked at it from a branding and positioning point of view. We did a quick global benchmark on what is typical tuition for executive training. We concluded that we were not extremely high and we were not extremely low.' For the internal team, Van Dijk realised the price point would put serious pressure on delivering quality, which he found appealing. To the outside world, it is equally a sign of ambition: 'It is a serious amount so participants will take us seriously.'

Partnerships with established strong brands helped. 'When we started, we had some stellar partners like McKinsey, Vodafone and OMA. We had the freedom of doing something completely new while having credibility through our association with something existing and trustworthy. It allowed us to build a position quickly.' But there wasn't yet anyone to make first referrals and testify to the quality of the programme. 'Our head of recruiting, Eduard, asked how he could ever sell THNK. We had absolutely nothing we could sell. So we said, "Why don't we have dinners with potential candidates. We will sit down and spend a great evening talking about their dreams, the problems they face, the challenges they want to overcome... Then we will explain how we can help them." We took the mindset of a venture capitalist or an A&R manager. We were looking for the talent that we wanted to invest in instead of recruiting people to fill our bench. That worked well with the kind of group we aimed to attract. They are so independent that anyone asking them questions about how they want to be supported is very welcome.'

In just a few years THNK has managed to build an impressive community of over 500 participants, including top executives, royalty, activists, government representatives and designers. How has the school done it? 'About 70% of participants are being referred to us by past participants. We track net promoter score and we follow it very diligently.' Keeping an eye on the mission has paid off over time too. 'THNK takes its own mission very, very seriously. Anything we do is about supporting creative leaders creating innovative solutions to large societal challenges. When you forget about the objectives of that mission, you become just sales-driven, or you are just trying to survive. As long as you hold on to your mission and you are serious about it, it constantly inspires you and is contagious to people around you. We get quite a lot of gifts in terms of partnerships, help, support and talented people because people identify with our mission.'

When potential participants research THNK, they find its presence online is catalysed mostly through content. 'The objective of sharing knowledge is that it builds knowledge. I don't look at it from a PR point of view, to position ourselves or to promote THNK; I look at it as developing sets of tools to the

MISSION COMPOSER

Trouble articulating your mission? This tool will take you through the process step-by-step, see page 174.

WE WERE GOING TO ASK THEM FOR A SERIOUS AMOUNT OF MONEY AND WE DID NOT HAVE A CURRICULUM YET, NOR A REPUTATION

benefit of our target group.' Van Dijk finds the general level of knowledge exchange in the area of innovation, creativity and entrepreneurship quite shallow. 'Most of the insights are based on anecdotes. All this admiration of Apple is fair and well deserved, but Apple is in many respects a complete outlier and you can only learn from it in terms of what an outlier does. We set quite a high bar for the stuff that we write. We want to protect that everyone understands it and we hope that pieces we write trigger debate and opposing views.' Letting your actions speak has been THNK's foremost brand building strategy. 'We don't believe in advertising. What we do believe in is creating pull. I am not sure it's the best approach for every enterprise but for us and for me, it's what makes me feel good. It's authentic. That's the way I want us to grow.'

To van Dijk, there is no difference between the brand and the business. 'One side is your brand and your brand positioning, your target group and the particular product or service that you offer. Then there is a whole delivery system, the quality of the people that you put into it, the faculty, the way you deliver things – all those elements have to be fully consistent; they feed each other.'

Van Dijk offers one point of advice to anyone starting a business. 'If you have some skill or talent which is distinctive, which is hardcore different, then in that particular space you know the difference between mediocrity and excellence. Therefore, as an entrepreneurial leader, you should assume that outside of that particular focus of excellence, you are yourself relatively mediocre. For example, if you start brainstorming your own company name, you are going to end up with a name that

is mediocre. And that is because that is not your own particular skill. You should have self-awareness where you are great and where by definition you are not great, where you are merely okay.'

BE EDGY WHERE YOU ARE EXCELLENT AND EXPECT EXCELLENCE OF OTHERS IN THE AREAS WHERE YOU ARE MERELY OKAY

RESULTS

Over 500 participants have completed the Executive Leadership programme and thousands more have taken part in THNK's in-company programmes. It is currently pursuing satellite locations in Dubai, Shanghai, São Paulo and Vancouver.

Use the advantage of being new. Be ruthlessly differentiating and build your brand on the best possible product, knowledge and experience you can deliver.

More on THNK
thnk.org
@THNK_org

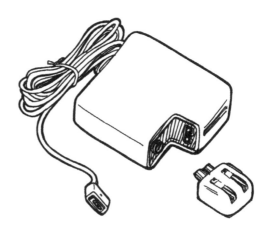

CASE: THE FINANCE BAR

FRUGAL IS THE
NEW COOL

How one woman with a bus is on a mission
to help people take charge of their personal
finances.

TAGGED: CONSULTANCY - COACHING - FINANCE -
NOT-FOR-PROFIT

In the US, many people are stuck in a swamp of lifelong debt. Worrying about the state of one's personal finances is far more prevalent than worrying about jobs, health or even food. Messaging around smart financial planning pales under the sunshine of the daily temptations from new cars to new shoes. Enter The Finance Bar founder Marsha Horton-Barnes, who is making frugal 'the new cool'.

When you think of responsible personal finance, what type of service comes to mind? The topic conjures up dusty offices, grey suits and plain misery. Personal finance expert Marsha Horton-Barnes saw that it could be done differently and founded The Finance Bar, a not-for-profit organisation advancing financial literacy. She believes that with commitment and discipline, anyone can turn their financial situation around.

Horton-Barnes clearly markets towards women. 'Women are often the people who reach out to me naturally, but also for 80% of the population, women handle the money in the household and therefore women became my focus.' Her biggest goal is to change women's mindset about money.

The brand hinges on the concept of being frugal, not an easy feat in a world that is out to seduce you every second of the day. 'A lot of people look at frugal as being cheap. I wanted to take the message of frugal as the new cool, to help women better understand that being frugal allows you to accomplish what you dream of in life, whether that means you have a balanced portfolio of investments, or savings that help you sleep at night. If you want to start your own business, that is what frugal can do for you. I always use myself as an example. Had I not been frugal, I would have never been able to launch The Finance Bar.'

Horton-Barnes has built a brand that effortlessly combines approachable personal finance coaching with a positive mindset and a feminine, stylish twist. 'I knew that the need for financial advice was there but I did not know yet what my service would look like. I knew that I did not want to set up a bricks-and-mortar shop because Charlotte, North Carolina is the second largest city for banking and there are financial planners everywhere. I wanted it to be different, something that people

planners everywhere. I wanted it to be different, something that people can really embrace. Food trucks and mobile fashion trucks are very popular here, and so one Sunday night I thought, "Why can't I put personal finance on a bus?"'

The old school bus made The Finance Bar mobile; the design had to make it loved. 'I envisioned that while I was talking to women on personal finance, I wanted them to feel at home, like it was their own personal space or their own cute office.

A LOT OF PEOPLE FEEL LIKE THEIR PERSONAL FINANCES ARE THE END OF THEM. I WANTED TO CONVEY THAT THE SUN WILL SHINE AGAIN!

So we created a very bright, girly colour scheme, used lots of pillows and a couch, and people can come in for coffee and tea. And it also represents me: I'm a bright and cheerful person and I want people to be able to identify with me.'

The brand is brought to life in dozens of lively ways. When you come in for a cup of coffee you will be sipping from a 'Frugal is the new cool' mug. If you are not in the neighbourhood (or in the country), you can download their super-easy-to-use expense app. Horton-Barnes blogs extensively with titles like 'The Beauty of Being Financially Responsible'. Through social media, campaigns encourage people to share their stories, and a growing group of followers eagerly take in the warm wisdom offered. Tapping into women's end-of-year financial stress and their love of detoxing, The Finance Bar offers a five day online Money Cleanse course during the holidays, helping you get your finances in order for the new year.

All the brand building concepts come from Horton-Barnes herself, with a little assistance from a designer. 'People are bombarded with messages all day telling them to buy things, and so I have to compete with that. I have to be creative about holding people's attention and keeping them focused on the long-term benefits of financial control.' The brand resonates with the audience because of one central point of departure: 'Any idea that I have for The Finance Bar I approach from the question of what would attract women? What are the things we really enjoy doing? One of the things women here in the US love is magazines. If you go to the local book store, you might not see a lot of people in the book aisles, but if you go to the magazine aisles, you will find a lot of women there. Women love bags, so we created these cute little bags with texts on them, which celebrate that women are now taking charge of their personal finances.'

It's a no-nonsense approach to reaching a large group of women drowning in personal debt. 'Treat yourself as an entrepreneur, not as a social entrepreneur, and think about what will resonate with the people you are trying to reach. If my target is to offer personal finance to women then I need to tap into what I know that women like.'

Perhaps the most powerful brand asset of The Finance Bar is Horton-Barnes herself. With an almost missionary zeal, a strong voice and a brand that is an extension of her personality, Horton-Barnes sets her sights on the horizon and gets people to follow her along the way. 'I knew in my gut that The Finance Bar met a need but I also knew that it was going to be a while before other people would embrace that. You have to believe in your message, in how you are trying to change the world. So do your research, know your market but know that it is going to be a while before people catch on. Don't forget to have a blast doing it, because that is what it is all about!'

RESULTS

Since its foundation in 2014, The Finance Bar has worked with over 10,000 students and more than 8,200 women face to face. The Finance Bar story has been featured on National Public Radio, Black Enterprise, Yahoo, Business Insider, Forbes and more.

Tap into what you know best and trust your instincts. Keep your target audience in mind and gear everything towards what would attract them.

More on The Finance Bar
thefinancebar.com
@thefinancebar

ACTION RANKING
One bus made a big difference to The Finance Bar. Organise your own brand building concepts by impact and feasibility through the tool on page 180.

CASE: SUGRU
FIX THE FUTURE

How one designer created a brand around
an entirely new material: mouldable glue.
Sugru is helping people everywhere to fix
and improve their stuff.

TAGGED: DIY · CREATIVITY · B2C

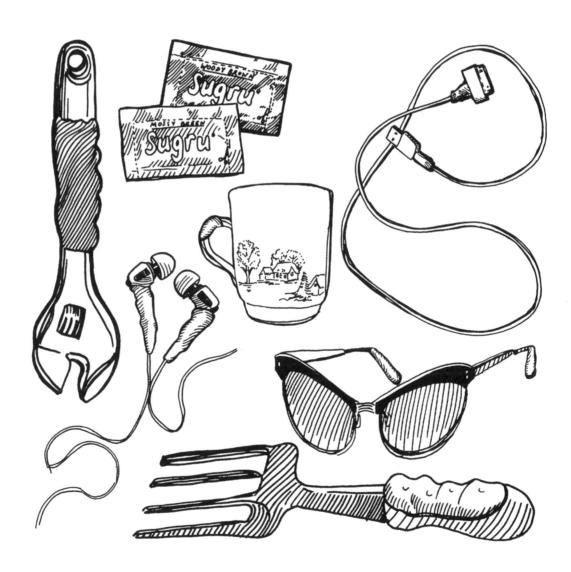

We live in a world where people throw away perfectly good stuff, from ski boots to desktop printers, just because small but crucial plastic parts of the products break and can't be replaced, or can't be replaced cost-effectively. While studying at the Royal College of Art in London, product designer Jane ni Dhulchaointigh experimented with different materials that would enable people to fix and improve their stuff. Over the course of six years she developed a mouldable glue that turns into a strong flexible rubber overnight. Through many ups and downs and dead ends in funding, production and business models, ni Dhulchaointigh turned Sugru into a booming consumer brand.

As the name Sugru (which means 'play' in Irish Gaelic) suggests, creativity is at the core of the brand. For a product that is in essence an industrial material, the company's founders have been extremely successful in creating an emotional connection with its audience. Though highly functional, Sugru is not a brand built on functional promises. Yes, it can fix the buckle on your ski boot, and it will keep your Apple laptop cord from fraying, but you can also use it to attach a camera to a helium balloon and send it to space, as a team of 11-year-old children did for a science challenge.

Sugru is on a mission to unleash people's creativity and apply it to fixing and enhancing their stuff. As ni Dhulchaointigh explains, 'Sugru is all about unlocking creativity, enabling people to fix and enhance things around them. It's about tackling the throwaway culture we live in and reimagining our surroundings to make them work harder for us. For me it was less about creating the product and more about creating the right tool and brand to inspire a new and more empowered culture around our "stuff". I'm so excited to find ways that help people discover their own creative potential to transform and improve anything.' The biggest brand ambassadors for Sugru are its users. Sugru can only come to life through their imagination, and the company invests heavily in sparking that imagination with examples. They hold in-store demonstrations, and ni Dhulchaointigh's partner and husband James features as the goofy guru in many of Sugru's inspirational videos, creating megalomaniac water pistols and throwing around child-proofed cameras.

SUGRU PUTS THE IDEAS AND INVENTIONS OF USERS FIRMLY IN THE SPOTLIGHT

It retweets, shares and likes people's creations, and features them on its website, encouraging them to make their own videos and posts about 'lifehacks' they have created using Sugru.

Initially, Sugru was a niche product adopted by the maker movement. 'We launched Sugru online without really knowing who our customers would be. We just wanted to find our people and inspire them with how Sugru could be part of their lives. In the first instance, we didn't really say what Sugru was for specifically; we talked about our mission and set out a challenge: "What will you do with this?" It worked like crazy to get some people excited. Creative people were really drawn to it and loved finding new uses for it, and that was hugely exciting for us in turn, because we started to really learn what it was good for, what it wasn't so good for, and what people used it for again and again, things like fixing household appliances, gadgets and shoes for example.'

With the brand going more and more mainstream, they are fast outgrowing their original niche. 'The thing to remember is that our mission has always been the same: to help inspire a creative, problem-solving culture in a mass-consumer way. We never wanted Sugru to be only for "creative people", but those people were key to our learning and building the brand in the early days, and they continue to help us reach more and more people who don't consider themselves to be creative but need to fix things up, and enjoy up-cycling, home improvement and so on. We evolved our tagline from "Hack things better" to "Fix that thing" to maintain that tone of a call to arms, but appeal to more people.'

Reaching that bigger audience is not easy. 'Taking a personal approach is part of making Sugru feel accessible and exciting for our users, but there can be downsides too. For example, some new customers may think we're smaller than we actually are, and therefore have trust questions over Sugru as a product: "Will it really work?" It's a tricky balance, but I think as long as we're focusing on achieving our mission, we'll do the right thing.' Fortunately, even as the audience becomes more and more diverse, one trait continues to hold it together. 'What they all have in common is that they enjoy getting hands on, and sorting things out for themselves!'

The branding of Sugru and design of the packaging has always been an integrated component of the strategy to attract more users. 'Because my and James's background as Sugru founders is in design, building the brand identity and creating the communications has been one of the things we've enjoyed the most. It's such a pleasure –and constant challenge!– to figure out what sort of design decisions will trigger the reactions we want from our users. We always see design as a means to an end, a tool for behaviour change. What do we have to do to capture curiosity? To build confidence? To inspire trust?' The development of the brand has been an ongoing evolution since 2009. 'The identity and packaging have evolved as the company has grown, because we keep learning. Our users keep teaching us! And because the context is changing and growing.'

'For example from around 2013 we had to start building the retail environment into our considerations more and more, to help Sugru stand out on the shelf and be understood without the help of all the rich media that can surround it online.'

Jane blogs and speaks extensively about Sugru's journey as a product and a company. 'We have been very transparent about our successes and challenges throughout the process of developing the product and building the Sugru brand, and we do that because we hope it demystifies the process of getting a project or business off the ground and will encourage more people to become "do-ers" whether with DIY projects, or starting a business or social venture.'

Sugru has big plans for the future. 'We want to be in that "fix all" kitchen drawer in everyone's home. Yet what drives us is one simple mission: to help people fix things and enjoy tapping into their creative potential to solve everyday problems. It is those "eureka" moments when someone fixes something

and shares their fix story online that drives the whole team. Whatever size we grow to, I hope that mission and drive will never change.'

RESULTS

Sugru is on the verge of becoming a household name in the UK and the US and not just for its usefulness. People love and trust the brand. In the summer of 2015, the brand crowdfunded £3.5 million in order to scale to the global market, overfunding the campaign by 355%. In 2017, the company again successfully crowdfunded £1.8 million.

When you have a good product, only your imagination stands in the way of making it great. Even a practical household product can become a brand people love and support.

More on Sugru
sugru.com
@sugru

THE MANIFESTO MAKER
Create a manifesto for your brand, like Sugru!
See page 190.

CASE: SOKO
FASHIONABLE, FAST AND FAIR

How an ethical fast-fashion company increases the incomes of artisans five times over through a brand women love to come back to time and time again.

TAGGED: ETHICAL FASHION - INNOVATION - TECH - ONLINE RETAIL

The artisan craft industry is the second largest employer in the developing world. Its workers are also some of the most disenfranchised. On average, women account for 80% of the workforce, but make only 10% of the income. Fashion brand/tech company Soko provides a way for artisans to improve their livelihoods by connecting them directly with market demand around the world through a first-generation mobile phone marketplace. This approach matches existing consumer behaviour with responsibly sourced products, proving that ethical small-scale production can feed the mainstream market.

THE BRANDING CASE

Nairobi is a hotbed for social innovation and tech, and it was here that Soko founders Ella Peinovich, Gwendolyn Floyd and Catherine Mahugu met and recognised their shared passion for artisanship and women's empowerment. Combining their talents for technology and systems design, they have invented a radically new way for fashion brands to source their products. When a Soko customer puts in an order it is sent to a digital marketplace that artisans in Kenya can access and respond to via their mobile phones, even if they lack access to the Internet, a computer, or a bank account. The artisans produce the jewellery, and Soko delivers it to the customer. Because there are no other middlemen, a Soko partnership can quadruple the income of the average artisan.

The road that led to today's success has had some twists and turns. Soko began as SasaAfrica, a tech company conceived as the 'Etsy of Africa', a digital marketplace that offered local artisans a platform to sell and market their own unique, one-off designs. 'The perceived value of the products didn't align with the actual value of the goods. We realised marketing and branding were very important,' Peinovich says. 'Also, the style of the jewellery was very ethnic,' adds Floyd, 'which only appealed to a niche market. We recognised a scalable market demand from wholesale consumers that would enable us to pivot our supply chain to a more robust end-to-end solution.'

During this initial phase, time and money were both in short supply, eaten up by the demands of maintaining and operating the tech platform and building their supplier and market bases.

The team started applying for funds and entering competitions, and SasaAfrica won the BiD Women in Business award, Rice Business Plan Competition, Global Social Entrepreneurship Competition (GSEC), the DEMO Lionesses and People's Choice awards at DEMO Africa, the ITV Telecom World Young Innovators Competition, a USAID Development Innovation Venture Grant and a Best Buy College Innovator Fund prize, getting over US$200,000 (€184,000) in seed funding, mentoring and coaching. The awards and funding also resulted in substantial early PR and a group of first fans who gave the founders crucial feedback. 'That is when we rebranded to Soko,' says Peinovich.

WE NEEDED AN UMBRELLA COMPANY THAT COULD RAISE THE KIND OF PRICES THAT COULD COVER THE COST OF MARKETING AND PROMOTION INVOLVED TO MEET THE MAINSTREAM CONSUMER

'We went from a technology company for artisans to a consumer-facing company. To make this possible we moved from unique pieces to a collection of items that could be produced in series, and then we offered them at wholesale.' The change quickly paid off. In 2015 Soko raised US$700,000 from a Dubai-based venture capital firm and from angel investors to help support further growth.

For a tech company to enter the extremely competitive world of online fashion retail is no small feat. The shift from a miscellaneous assortment of artisan-designed pieces to a coordinated collection was particularly significant. 'We are lucky that both Ella and I are trained designers,' says Floyd, 'so when we made that switch it was easy for me to pick up the product design, and I now design several hundred pieces each year over the course of six weeks.' Soko's collection offers quick delivery, an attractive price point and contemporary aesthetics that score major points with upmarket stores in the West like Nordstrom and Anthropologie. As Floyd says, 'We sell ethical fast fashion and have a product that is very on-trend, demand-responsive and very affordable and ethically produced. So we were able to corner that niche fairly easily because no one else is able to do that in the way we are able to through our technology. We can actually compete on timelines with Zara and H&M, but we are ethically and sustainably sourced. Plus, our story is really differentiating.'

Peinovich considers a differentiating brand proposition absolutely vital, an aspect that she sees a lot of social-impact companies ignore. 'If you are producing life-saving devices make them as cheap as possible, but if you are marketing a service or product where you need to differentiate yourself in the market, it is extremely important to create an aspirational brand.' That aspirational aspect includes the stories of the artisans themselves. At first, they featured prominently on the website, but Soko has adopted a new approach that creates an even more direct connection between the customer and the artisan: each piece of jewellery ships with the story of the woman who crafted it, linking customers emotionally to the things they wear and the people who made them.

Floyd says that the products sell themselves with very little outside help. 'Most starting fashion brands will reinvest 50% of a month's revenue back into branding and marketing for the next month, over the course of three years in order to gain a foothold in the market. The only marketing we've been involved in has been going to trade shows, and very limited e-commerce activities. To date, we've mostly grown through wholesale. To stores like Nordstrom, we offer a great story that they themselves cannot offer.'

This smart approach to entering the market helped to avoid huge investments in brand building in the early years. Most brands start with e-commerce to be able to position themselves in the market and then go for wholesale. Soko did it the other way around.

WE HAVE FOUND SUCCESS IN BUILDING OUR BRAND THROUGH WHOLESALE, WHICH IN THE END IS MORE COST-EFFECTIVE

Soko, of course, does not exist in a vacuum, and although its brand proposition helps it to stand out in the context of a luxury department store, it still has to compete with big-name brands wielding big-name budgets. Top-quality in-store displays help Soko to project the same aura of quality and glamour as their bigger competitors.

Another strategy for brand recognition involves partnerships. Soko has teamed up with Pencils of Promise, an innovative educational not-for-profit, and a collaboration with a well-known handbag brand is also being negotiated.

A third crucial factor is style. Floyd works hard to ensure that Soko's collection is more than just fair trade items handmade from sustainable materials by Kenyan women; the jewellery, ranging from minimalist to statement pieces, must have a wide, contemporary appeal. 'Most jewellery that is made in Africa looks really niche, or goes for the boho style, and we think that we can use the heritage practices and materials to create accessories that appeal to all women. We are not nichifying either at price point or in aesthetic. People get really excited when we say that we really want to bring these goods to the mainstream market, because it means that we can really change how things are sourced in this industry. It also means that everyday people can afford something with a story, something of value and that is sustainably sourced.'

In other words, Soko offers women looking to buy ethical fashion a great product without having to compromise on style. Floyd: 'Because I am the principal designer, there has been a really unified aesthetic that also translates to other parts of the brand.' The simple, chic jewellery with an ethnic edge is combined with clean typography and dreamy, city-meets-savannah photography. Gorgeous models show off the pieces with class, which emphasises that the price of the jewellery is not just a charitable donation to a worthy cause, but a way to treat yourself to a bit of high style.

NOT ALL WOMEN IN SOKO'S TARGET AUDIENCE ARE SENSITIVE TO THE SAME TRIGGERS

Floyd points out: 'Young professional women in the middle of their twenties and thirties love the brand. They are interested in innovation; they think the story is cool. Then there are the people who want to help the poor, and the people who want to redefine the narrative of such people as actual agents of change, as entrepreneurs that we are partnering with. So every group is different and we are still fine-tuning how we talk to each of them.'

Soko is also working hard to build its brand at the other end of the operation; its explosive growth means that there is an ever-growing need for skilled artisans. 'We have to market to both,' Peinovich says, 'and that creates a really unique dynamic. It's an economic divide, technological divide, geographical divide, cultural divide; we are trying to create a bridge to develop one entity in the middle, which has now grown to provide high-quality goods to the wholesalers and production facilitation and supply chain solutions to the artisans.' Thanks to word-of-mouth and the promise of a substantial increase in income, marketing to the artisans is not so much a question of convincing people to join as it is of ensuring that they all work at the speed and level of quality that Soko needs.

Peinovich explains, 'What we are working on now is creating what we call "stickiness" and loyalty to what is actually a distributed network of artisans. They are independent, How do you ensure that they commit to the orders? It's an alignment thing. We are not the easiest customers to work for in that we expect very high quality and we work on relatively short

timelines. In return, we support them with asset financing, we provide them with tools, we do training, we have deposits on our orders upfront so they produce without having upfront cost. There are great benefits to being part of our network. As far as our branding with artisans is concerned, there is a certain amount of "proof in the pudding" needed before artisans may be willing to change their speed or standard of work to be the right match with us –it's a behaviour change. At this point we serve over 1,000 artisans, we have over 110 workshops that we work with. To grow our relationship with artisans we have field officers who are our ambassadors.'

With the social impact of their venture clearly paying off, Soko is proving that ethical fast fashion can compete with traditional unsustainable and unethical practices. 'We always knew that Soko was going to be a globally operating catalyst for supply chain innovation,' Peinovich says. 'That has never changed. Even through all the pivots of the company, we are still catalysing what it means to work with and do business with the developing world. We just recognise that we have a bigger part to play in this consumer landscape.'

Looking to the future, Soko seeks to expand geographically as well as to reach out to new groups of women. Peinovich: 'We don't have the level of attraction of a household name just yet. We have a lot of really early adopters. I think that really early consumers, they get the social impact. They want to see a change; they can understand that they can wield their consumer power for good. They understand you can buy ethical and buy beautiful.' Sometimes other ethical fashion brands approach Peinovich and comment on their being in competition with each other, but she doesn't see it that way at all. 'We are a fashion company that believes ethical is the new status quo. We are in competition with the companies that produce cheaply in China under disgraceful conditions. That is the market we are taking over.'

RESULTS

Soko currently connects 2,100 African artisans to customers worldwide. On average, participation in the Soko marketplace has increased the artisan's household income five-fold. In 2014, the average Soko artisan sold 1,090 pieces, a total of 41,309 items. To date, Soko has channelled over $1 million to artisans. The brand is active in 35 countries and for sale at Nordstrom and Anthropologie and through its own online store.

In order to achieve the large-scale impact that Soko was looking for, a radical change in business plan and branding of the products was necessary. Reaching a mass audience and conquering a part of a very competitive market can require investment of up to 50% of your monthly revenue in marketing.

More on Soko
shopsoko.com
@Shop_Soko

CHAPTER 3
THE ANATOMY OF A BRAND

BRANDS ARE BUILT LIKE HUMANS

Brands are constructed much like humans are. You have an inner core: your character, personality, set of beliefs, what you want to achieve in your life.

This expresses itself through your identity: what you look like, what you say, how you say it. Your core and your identity shape your interactions with the outer world and how people think and feel about you, from the tweets you send, to the events you attend or organise, to the friends you surround yourself with, to the things you do (or don't do) for others. The signals people get on the outside help them form an opinion on what is on the inside.

This is exactly what you are doing as a brand: you want to build relationships with your audiences. You want them to prefer you and be loyal to you in order to grow your social or environmental impact and business. You need to have a core that drives you, an identity that makes you recognisable and interactions that create a relationship between you and your audience.

Everyone can benefit from understanding the holistic brand model that underpins strong brands. When you know the anatomy of a strong brand, the whole and the parts, you can use it to your advantage.

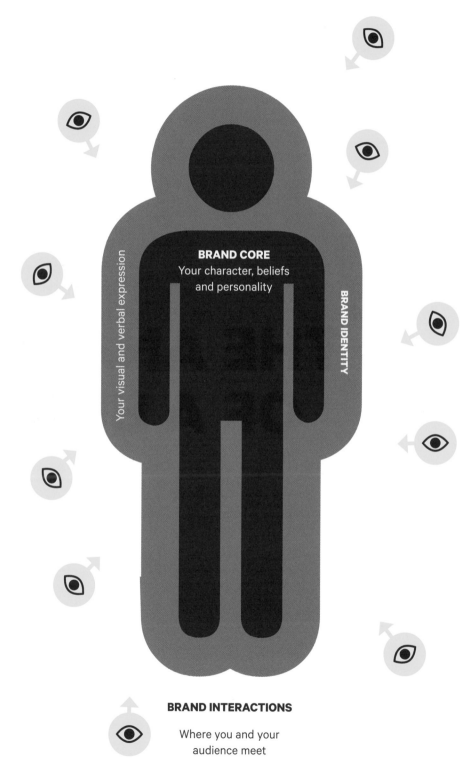

Your visual and verbal expression

BRAND CORE
Your character, beliefs and personality

BRAND IDENTITY

BRAND INTERACTIONS

Where you and your audience meet

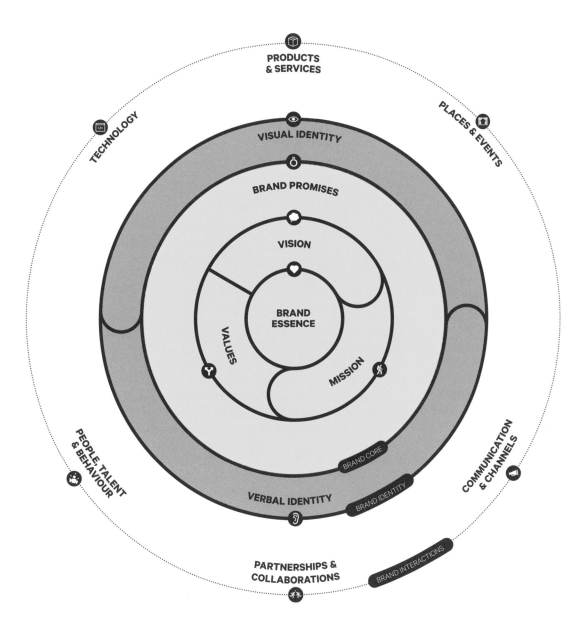

In order to make it easier to construct a holistic brand, we've created a model we call the Brand Thinking Canvas. Its power lies in helping you understand the anatomy of a strong brand and what it takes to successfully direct how people think and feel about you across six main interaction points with your audiences. The core, identity and interactions all break down into their own separate components.

THE BRAND CORE The brand core is built on the change you want to see in the world. Why you do what you do and what your road to change is. The core is captured in a vision, mission and values. Your brand promises to capture what you commit to deliver to your audiences.

THE BRAND IDENTITY consists of your visual and verbal expression: what you look like, how you talk.

BRAND INTERACTIONS guide all the points of contact that you build with your audiences. From the people you hire and how they behave when encountering your customers, to the partnerships you form with others, to the types of channels you choose to communicate to the places where you want to be seen, to the products and services you offer. Your core guides how you set up your production chain or source your materials.

On the next pages, we will go deeper into what each layer and component means for your brand, and we'll look at practical examples from real-world brands.

The Brand Core

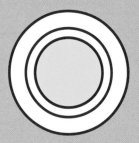

The core of the brand is the foundation that we build on. Every element in the core is built around the questions 'Who', 'What' and 'Why'. Examining the brand core of mission, vision and values is a great way for changemakers to think about how they express what they want to achieve, for whom and by what means. Some people literally put their vision, mission and values on a web page to communicate them with the world. Other people weave it into the fabric of their brand and are more of the 'show, don't tell' kind. Whether you choose to make it explicit or implicit, your brand core represents the driving force behind everything you do.

WHAT IT ENCOMPASSES

- Brand essence.
- Vision.
- Mission.
- Values.
- Brand promises.

WHAT IT'S FOR

- Defining the driving force of your brand.
- Creating a shared sense of purpose.
- Setting criteria that aid decision making.
- Catalysing strong ideas for brand expressions.
- Briefing third parties.
- Shaping content for communication, presentations and pitches.

BRAND ESSENCE

This is your brand's reason for being, expressed in the simplest, most compelling sentence you can manage. A strong brand essence becomes the departure point for everything you do, the hook on which you can hang every idea, the catalyst for new products and services, the basis of your communication strategy, the criterion for selecting partners, etc.

A brand essence is tough to develop. It can take years of distilling and rearranging or it can be the result of a 'eureka' moment. Whether you are branding a product, a service, a philosophy or a movement, a strong brand essence is one of the most powerful assets you have, so keep working at it!

Take for example Japanese lifestyle brand Muji. In our busy modern lives, there is an overdose of impulses. Muji believes that creating simplicity around us with a few quality items creates a better mental balance. It offers a line of furniture, kitchen products, clothing, storage products and office materials in a characteristic, super-minimalist Japanese style.

The Muji brand is centred on the philosophy *hari hachi bu*, the Japanese practice of eating until you are 80% full to benefit health and well-being.

This essence is translated to a brand that drives everything Muji does. It is translated to the products, which are created using the simplest possible form and least possible amount of materials. It is translated to the brand identity: no Muji brand label can be found on any of the products. Communication is kept to a bare minimum. Muji images and texts are tranquil and practical. Their stores are functional and minimalist, and their team is religious about keeping the stores tidy and organised.

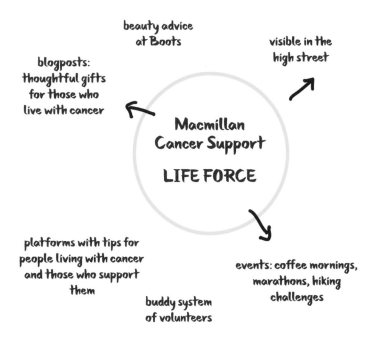

talkshow

movie
productions

bookclub

broadcasting
network

angel
network

Oprah
Winfrey
LIVE YOUR
BEST LIFE

magazine

partners:
Dr. Phil, Dr. Oz
(mental, physical health)
Suze Orman
(money matters)

spirituality
health
personal development
health, style

leadership
academy
for girls

bootcamp

coaching

classes

summer
school

psychotherapy

tools for a
thoughtful life:
books, games, kits,
art, stationery

The School Of Life

EMOTIONAL
INTELLIGENCE

wisdom on how
to live life well:
YouTube
videos +
Twitter

schools in city
centres in shopping
spaces

collaborations
with Tate

founder:
philosopher Alain de
Botton + trainers &
well-known writers

VISION

Everything starts with a vision. A vision describes the change you want to see in the world; it is how you describe WHY you do what you do, to what end. For people to follow you, they must understand where it is that you are going.

What does the world you want to see look like? If you want to lead change, you have to be able to paint people a picture of where you want to take them, whether you are talking to team members, customers, investors or producers. People need to know why you do the things you do so they can contribute to it in the best way possible. Whether you are an individual, a movement, or a large organisation, having a clear vision is crucial.

DIFFERENT LENSES

Each person and organisation has its own goals and its own idea of what success is. A vision can be crafted through different lenses: your impact on people ('a world without poverty'), on the planet ('a world that provides all people with the nourishment they need'), or on your industry ('a nature conservation sector that thrives through smart applications of technology.')

REACHING TOO HIGH?

The gap between an idealistic vision and daily reality can be uncomfortable. Kevin Sweeney, former Marketing and Communications Director of the outdoor brand Patagonia, says, 'In any entity where ideology is involved, there is a disparity between ideology and reality. A potential pitfall is that this gap will always be the subject of intense conversation. This can be constructive or destructive. A positive vision is much more impactful. What is important is to create a vision: what the country could be like, what a company could be like. It's a rare skill, but when it's done well, it's magic.'

THE CLIMB
People often get their mission and vision confused. This tool on page 172 makes it easy to tell them apart.

VISION VISUALISATION
Do you find it a challenge to create an exciting, unique vision? Jumpstart your brain by visualising it. See page 189.

FORMULA

Looking at vision statements of organisations in a completely different area than you yourself are active in can be very helpful. They can provide a formula for your own vision.

VISION EXAMPLES

SolarCity wants to see a world where renewable energy is cheaper than fossil fuels.

The Mustard Seeds Organisation believes in a Dandora that is clean, green, healthy and safe for all its residents. Not a slum, but an estate!

ColorOfChange wants to see a US where all Americans are represented, served and protected regardless of race or class.

Habitat for Humanity is working towards a world where everyone has a decent place to live.

Creative Commons seeks to realise the full potential of the Internet —universal access to research and education, full participation in culture— to drive a new era of development, growth, and productivity.

Internet of Elephants wants to see 20 million people wake up in the morning to check their smartphones and see how their elephant is doing.

Designathon Works is striving for a world where all children's creativity is cultivated to use technology for a better world.

SpaceX wants to see 1 million people on Mars.

MISSION

What do you do to realise your vision? A mission describes what you do to work towards your idea for change.

Mission-driven organisations perform better because they know what they deliver and why. The simpler and more memorable the mission, the more clearly it can guide you and your team's activities and get others to support you in your pursuit of change. Like your vision, a mission statement can be framed from different perspectives. You can have a mission to change your industry ('to be an advocate for the use of technology in wildlife conservation'), to change the world ('to create games that help people live happier and healthier lives') or to achieve a specific ambition ('to design educational programmes that are used and loved by one million parents worldwide').

KEEP IT SHORT

Kevin Starr, the Managing Director of the Mulago Foundation, which offers funding to social enterprises thinks mission statements should never be longer than eight words. 'As investors in impact, we don't want to wade through a bunch of verbiage about "empowerment", "capacity-building" and "sustainability". We want to know exactly what you're trying to accomplish. We want to cut to the chase with a simple eight-word formula: a verb, a target population, and an outcome that implies something to measure, and we want it in eight words or less.' Starr finds eight words long enough to be specific and short enough to force clarity. 'Rehabilitate coral reefs in the Western Pacific'. 'Prevent mother-child transmission of HIV in Africa'. 'Get Zambian farmers out of poverty'. Those are the kinds of impact the Mulago Foundation wants to fund.

THE MISSION COMPOSER
Trouble articulating your mission? This tool on page 174 will take you through the process step-by-step.

MISSION EXAMPLES

Google intends to organise the world's information and make it universally accessible and useful.

Acumen raises charitable donations to invest in companies, leaders, and ideas that are changing the way the world tackles poverty.

GirlEffect works to change the world for girls, so girls can change the world.

Nest reinvents unloved but important house products.

SolarCity aims to accelerate mass adoption of sustainable energy.

ColorOfChange is strengthening black America's political voice using the Internet. The movement keeps members informed and gives them ways to act on pressing issues facing black people in America.

The School of Life is devoted to developing emotional intelligence, offering a variety of programmes and services concerned with how to live wisely and well.

ClientEarth mobilises activist lawyers committed to securing a healthy planet.

Factory45 is fighting fast fashion one entrepreneur at a time.

SpaceX revolutionises space technology, with the ultimate goal of enabling people to live on other planets.

Warby Parker offers designer eyewear at a revolutionary price, while leading the way for socially conscious businesses.

MD Anderson Cancer Center is working to eradicate cancer.

Patagonia seeks to build the best products while causing no unnecessary harm and using its business to inspire and implement change.

VALUES

Human beings are driven by values, principles instilled in us through family and culture when we are young. They can be individual values or group values. The French Revolution, for instance, was driven by 'liberty, equality, fraternity'. Though our value sets may grow and develop throughout our lives, they are some of the most consistent aspects of our personality.

Like people, organisations have values, whether or not they are explicitly (or accurately) stated. Organisations with strong values perform better because their values provide a clear guiding compass for the future and make it easier to make choices. Values are also often the most consistent aspect of their natures. Markets can change, conditions can change, but organisations tend to stay true to these basic principles that guide our thinking and behaviour. An organisation's values create a distinct personality and company culture. Values are the one thing you need to capture well when your organisation grows beyond the size of a soccer team.

THE FOUNDER LEADS

If an organisation is founded by an authentic personality, his or her values trickle down into an organisational culture and make their way into each team member's belief system organically. Sometimes, however, these founders leave or take a back seat, and everyone in the company has to be able to take individual ownership of the organisation's operating principles.
The founder's organic value system has to be made explicit to ensure that the company consistently makes the right decisions.

A BAD REP

Values form a prominent element of branding but audiences take them more or less seriously depending on what they see an organisation actually do. Some of the banks at the heart of the economic crisis of the late 2000s touted values such as integrity, trustworthiness, and social consciousness.

DEFINING VALUES

Defining your values requires you to turn on your bullshit radar. Which universal beliefs do you hold? Are these values really the guide to everything you do? What are the concrete, everyday ways in which you put them into practice? If the values you espouse don't guide your actions, they simply aren't your real values. Expanding on a value by crafting your own, tailor-made definition can help you clarify what you really believe.

IDEO'S VALUES IN ACTION

Be optimistic: believing that something is possible somehow makes it so.

Collaborate: the most powerful asset we have in our arsenal is the word 'we'.

Embrace ambiguity: get comfortable with uncomfortable-ness.

Learn from failure: ask for forgiveness, not for permission.

Make others successful: going out of your way to help others succeed is the secret sauce.

Take ownership: the unwritten social contract here: individual ownership supports collective responsibility. Own that.

Talk less, do more: nothing is a bigger buzz-kill than over-intellectualising. Design is about rolling up your sleeves and making things.

THE VALUES GAME
Investigate and challenge how you (will) put your values into practice, and what they mean for everything you do and say. See page 194.

LIVE YOUR VALUES

Values only work in building a strong brand if they are at the heart of every decision you and your team will make. When values are only words on paper, or applied to only one aspect of your activities, situations can arise where your actions or communications misalign with your values. This makes you less believable and less impactful.

For instance, many organisations with a development or sustainability mission are producing massive numbers of t-shirts, banners, notebooks, key cords and pens with their logo on them, to give away as gifts and/or to build brand recognition and visibility. More often than not, these items are produced under bad working conditions and with harmful materials.

To critical audiences (potentially your most fervent advocates or loyal employees), missteps like these can damage how they think and feel about you.

Review HR policies, supply chains, partnerships and communications regularly to ensure they are aligned with what you stand for.

WHEN VALUES FAIL

These three examples demonstrate what happens when values are not integrated into all aspects of the brand's activities and decision making.

A large telecom brand has defined its values in the boardroom: they are personal, transparent, and stand for secure innovation. In their stores, however, customers have to pick a number and wait in line for 40 minutes only to be told that they cannot get advice on a new data plan because the shop has no access to their personal information.

An NGO in economic development is passionate about economic empowerment. It needs photographic material for its communications portraying refugees in the Middle East. A photo agency that pays the people portrayed in their photos a royalty is slightly more expensive than a photo agency that only pays the photographer for the work. The NGO chooses the cheaper option.

A leading bank got its start a century ago by investing in local small-scale businesses which transformed communities. It changes its corporate values to once again include solidarity with local entrepreneurs. However, the bank reviews its employees' performance based only on financial targets. Therefore there is no incentive for the employees to approve loans to more risky small businesses. The bank's HR policy undermines its values.

SOCIETY & RELATIONSHIPS: HOW WE VIEW OURSELVES AND OTHERS

Empathy
Self-reliance
Tolerance
Compassion
Collaboration
Respect
Trust
Forgiveness
Inclusiveness
Sharing
Reciprocity
Diversity
Unity
People-centred
User-centred
Transparency
Altruism

MORALITY: OUR SENSE OF RIGHT AND WRONG

Justice
Equality
Honesty/Sincerity
Integrity
Fairness

ATTITUDE: HOW WE VIEW THE WORLD

Inquisitiveness
Ambition
Determination
Resourcefulness
Optimism

Open-mindedness
Fearlessness/Courage
Exploration
Humility
Pragmatism
Adaptability
Agility
Gratitude
Loyalty
Creativity
Commitment
Flexibility

POWER: HOW WE VIEW AUTHORITY AND CHANGE

Challenging
Equality
Innovation
Independence

IDENTITY: HOW WE VIEW OUR PLACE IN THE WORLD

Authenticity
Balance
(Un)conventionalism
Individuality
Expression

IDEOLOGY: HOW WE VIEW PEOPLE AND THE ENVIRONMENT

Non-violence
Impartiality
Activism
Sustainability
Do-no-harm
Solidarity

Brotherhood
Universality
Emancipation
Citizenship
Non-partisanship
Neutrality
Freedom/Liberty
Accessibility
Openness

BUSINESS: WHAT DRIVES WHAT WE DO AND HOW WE DO IT

Ambition
Accountability
Excellence
Professionalism
Quality
Service
Entrepreneurship
Disruption/Challenge
Expertise
Knowledgeability
Craftsmanship
Leadership
Growth
Impact

QUALITY: WHAT WE BELIEVE TO BE GOOD

Excellence
Professionalism
Expertise
Craftsmanship
Beauty

PHILOSOPHY: HOW WE EVALUATE OUR LIVES AND OUR WORLD

Simplicity
Holistic/Connectivity
Rationality
Intuition
Aestheticism/Beauty
Solution-driven
Action-driven

CULTURAL VALUES

Be inspired by cultural values from across the world! For instance, the Seven Virtues of Bushido, which make up the code of the Japanese Samurai, are beautiful examples of deeply ingrained values that deliver meaning to the warriors' code. They are: *gi* (integrity), *rei* (respect), *yu* (heroic courage), *meiyo* (honour), *jin* (compassion), *makoto* (honesty and sincerity) and *chu* (duty and loyalty).

BRAND PROMISES

What do you commit to deliver to your audiences? What value do you add for them? How do you make their lives easier, better, richer, more beautiful? How do you empower them? What do you help them accomplish? Those are your brand promises.

Brand promises can be functional or emotional. And what you promise to deliver needs to be as differentiating from any sort of competition as possible.

Brand promises are the answer to the question that your audience will constantly ask when considering whether or not to engage with you: 'What's in this for me?' In the brand promises your offer is presented to the audience at its best value.

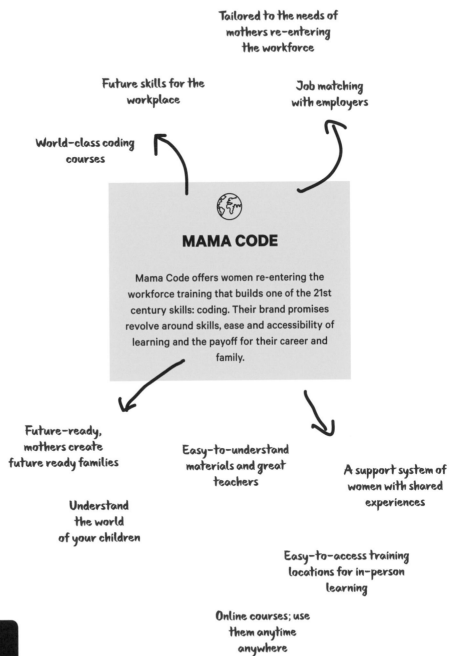

Tailored to the needs of
mothers re-entering
the workforce

Future skills for the
workplace

Job matching
with employers

World-class coding
courses

MAMA CODE

Mama Code offers women re-entering the workforce training that builds one of the 21st century skills: coding. Their brand promises revolve around skills, ease and accessibility of learning and the payoff for their career and family.

Future-ready,
mothers create
future ready families

Easy-to-understand
materials and great
teachers

A support system of
women with shared
experiences

Understand
the world
of your children

Easy-to-access training
locations for in-person
learning

Online courses; use
them anytime
anywhere

THE LADDER
Use this tool to take the step from a functional to an emotional promise. Go to page 184.

Brand Identity

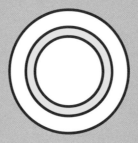

Organisations, like people, have personalities that are defined by character on the inside. An identity translates this inside to the outside. It is the expression of who you are and what you stand for. You can express yourself through words (verbal identity) and visuals (visual identity). The goal of developing a brand identity is to be recognisable, memorable and, hopefully, loveable. The visual and verbal are combined to create communication that is the face and the voice of your brand. In every expression, whether it's an ad campaign, or a business card, or the keynote presentation by the CEO at a conference, your audience recognises you. Different brands express their identity in different ways. Some identities are playful, others masculine and strong. Some brands are sassy, others are purely professional. A great identity should fit you like a tailor-made suit.

WHAT IT ENCOMPASSES

- Name and payoff/slogan/descriptor.
- Tone of voice (how you say it).
- Editorial angle (what you talk about, how you talk about it).
- Sound.
- Logo, typography & colour.
- Image concept: photography/ illustration/
- iconography/infographic style.
- Layout principles (grid, composition).
- Dynamic principles (animation, film).

WHAT IT'S FOR

- Translating your inner character, beliefs and personality to the outside world.
- Creating a recognisable, differentiating face and voice for your organisation/ product/service/cause.

Two people, two characters, two identities. They dress to suit their individual personalities and, whether intentionally or unintentionally, they make statements to their audiences on how they want to be perceived. They look different and speak differently. A good brand identity does exactly the same thing; it takes what lives on the inside and makes it visible (and audible) on the outside.

VERBAL IDENTITY

The words you choose to use are extremely important in guiding how you think about your brand, and what your audience thinks about what you do.

WORDS HAVE THE POWER TO UNLEASH CHANGE

From blood diamonds to dolphin-free tuna, words have the power of naming and shaming particular harmful practices. On the other hand, they also help capture and promote philanthropic business models like buy-one-give-one.

Especially in terms of changemaking, where existing practices are questioned and new categories are created, creativity and strategy are important when it comes to the words you use.

Words can work for you on many levels, from the name people know you by, to a manifesto that can bring like-minded people together. Words can make you memorable, understandable, relatable and personable. Words can make a concept that never existed before come to life. Some names become so well known, they become verbs (Google) or the name for an entire product category (Thermos, Aspirin).

In the following pages, we break down what a verbal identity consists of.

NAMING

Every starting company, NGO, movement, service or product needs a name. Naming your brand is one of the hardest decisions in the brand development process. If you have the mind of a poet or a linguist, or friends with great creative minds, the right name might just fall into your lap. Others leave it to professionals like branding agencies, specialised naming agencies or independent namers. Naming is a skill not to be taken lightly. Some experts work purely with their own poetic gifts, others get help from software. Regardless of the method, in a single naming process dozens or thousands of names can be proposed, considered, developed and discarded.

WHAT MAKES A GOOD NAME?

Because a name is so close to who you are, and you will have to see and say it dozens of times a day, choosing a name is serious business. When considering a name, ask yourself the following questions:

» Is it unique and memorable?
» Does it give an indication of what industry or category the product or service is in, what it does, or what makes it different?
» Can the name be trademarked?
» Are the online domain and the social media handles acceptable (the same as the name, or with a minimum of tricks like adding hyphens or suffixes)?
» Does it have positive connotations in the markets and countries that you will be active in?
» Is it easy to spell when you hear it?
» Is it timeless? Can it survive at least the next ten years?
» Can it be mistaken for something else when you hear it?

There are no guarantees that the name you choose is right. Some names have been complete failures. Other names would have not passed the test of negative connotations, but became a success through the success of the product itself. Think of Gap (a clothing retailer that sounds like an empty space) and the iPad (the electronic tablet computer that reminds us of a sanitary product). Seasoned naming experts will tell you there are few names that will fulfil all the criteria, but that at the end of the day, a great gut feeling about the name is a clear sign.

TRENDS

Fit2000, Fit4You, Fitly: naming is an area very much subject to trends. Resist the urge to pick up on a naming trend! Chances are that two years from now this fad will be passé, and you will be stuck with it (if your venture survives).

LEGAL CONSIDERATIONS

Remember that this process is not just a matter of finding a great name; it is also a question of finding a great name that is available. Names can be protected by trademarks, and your 'perfect' one may already be taken. Or it may be available, but the domain names and social media handles are taken. Do your research before you start using a name. When you find one that is available, trademark it.

DIY NAME TESTING

If you decide to develop a name without consulting a naming expert, be sure to conduct (confidential) surveys with different target groups: the general public, potential clients, users or investors, people in the industry, and if possible, people from foreign countries. Don't ask broad, vague questions like 'What do you think of this name?' Instead, ask questions like 'What do you think this company does?' or 'What associations do you have with this name?' Check their answers against the criteria on the previous page. If you find a great name be sure to do a legal and domain name check. In many cases, you will have to scrap your favourites because they are not available.

PAYOFF

A payoff, also known as a tag line, descriptor, catchphrase, motto or a slogan, is often seen in close company with your brand name and gives a little extra information about what you do or what you offer. It can be descriptive, emotional or aspirational. Payoffs can help people understand the category that you are in. Some payoffs are aspirational and encourage us to see a bigger picture. Adding a descriptive sentence can help to support a fictional brand name.

FUNCTIONAL OR FICTIONAL?

Imagine if personal genetics company 23andMe was called 'Genes Shop'? Choosing a functional or a fictional name has a huge impact on the personality that you show to the outside world.

FUNCTIONAL NAMES
+ clearly communicate what you do
+ help your audience to frame you in the right category
- are more difficult to protect legally
- will stand out less from the competition

FICTIONAL NAMES
+ are more differentiating and easier to trademark
+ have more emotion and personality that audiences can relate to
- take more time to embed in the minds of your audience
- can be hard to spell, pronounce or find online

PROTECTING YOUR BRAND
Read more about protecting your name and logo in the guest essay by Marleen Splinter on page 206.

Blogger: push button publishing
THNK: School for Creative Leadership
Chirps: eat what bugs you
Sugru: the future needs fixing

NAMES TO REMEMBER

Sugru
Mouldable glue that turns into rubber (the name, based on the Irish word for 'play', came to the inventor five years into product development).

Retronaut
Curators of historic photographic material that brings the past to life.

The School of Life
Workshops, books and events to help you develop your emotional intelligence.

23andMe
A personal genetics company, referring to the 23 chromosomes in our DNA.

UK Uncut
A grassroots movement taking action to highlight alternatives to austerity in Great Britain.

BRCK
A robust, mobile Wi-Fi device designed for rural and urban Africa.

LeanIn
A catchphrase by Sheryl Sandberg (to encourage women to 'lean in' at leadership levels), that turned into a book, a foundation and a movement.

Chirps
Chips made with cricket flour.

1776
An American incubator that supports entrepreneurs solving the world's greatest challenges (the number refers to the year of the American revolution).

Second Shot
East London café bringing people together and tackling homelessness one espresso at a time.

Hollaback!
An international movement to end harassment of women in public places.

Spare Fruit
Transforming rescued fruit into delicious 100% fruit crisps.

SuperBetter
Turns the road to better mental health into a game.

Viagra
Medication used to treat erectile dysfunction; the name is a combination of 'Niagara Falls' and 'vigour'.

TONE OF VOICE

The way you speak, the words you choose, the personality revealed through what you say: all these things define your tone of voice. It's all about attitude; a great tone of voice has a point of view! Some brands are formal, others more playful. Some brands question, others empower. Some speak an international language, others have a strong local appeal.

A brand's personality should be so strong that it comes to life through smart and surprising word choices or an interesting, unusual angle on topics. Your words deliver more than just your message; they say a great deal about the type of organisation you are. Applied properly, they can help you build strong relationships with your audiences.

A tone of voice can also be very literally brought to life by a particular person, through radio commercials or video voice-overs. The voice you choose, its gender, cultural background and accent all communicate something about you as a brand.

NOT SO INNOCENT

Few brands have such a distinct tone of voice as Innocent, a smoothie company from the UK. The team of three students that founded the company included a writer in their branding process from their very first steps, and the tone of voice is arguably their most defining brand asset, perhaps even the best in the business. Innocent's voice works wonders on product shelves, in campaigns, on social media and beyond.

On Valentine's Day: 'If you were a post on Facebook, I wouldn't want to share you with anyone.'

'How do they all fit in the bottle? We use our special shrinking ray.'

On the cartons: 'This recipe is a bit special. We've squeezed three of the world's finest superfruits into it, a combination of pomegranate, blueberry and acai. Tastes great and much better than getting busy with a funnel and a piece of hosepipe.'

On the website: 'Hello, we're Innocent. We're here to make it easy for people to do themselves some good.'

At the bottom of the smoothie carton: 'You should probably try to open this carton at the other end. Not that we are telling you how to run your life or anything, but it seems to work much easier when the drink comes out of the spout on top.'

Headline of a press release: "Some thoughts from us on the Paris climate-change agreement.'

EDITORIAL ANGLE

What topics do you talk about? Through what lens do you look at the world? An editorial angle based on your brand's core helps when creating content for your presentations, PR, blog posts, and marketing.

STORY

Every brand has a story: who it was founded by, why it came into the world, what adventures happened on the road to where it is today. Being able to articulate that story in a human, engaging way helps people relate to you. Incorporating your audience's stories into your own story can help build strong relationships.

 TELLING STORIES
Read more about what storytelling can do for you in the guest essay by Roshan Paul on page 200.

VISUAL IDENTITY

Your visual identity is literally the face of your organisation. When you cannot be present somewhere physically, your visual identity will take your place. It is one of the most powerful tools you have for creating recognition over time. An identity that has visual impact will help you stand out from the crowd.

SHOW, DON'T TELL
A visual identity helps you to communicate your personality in an intuitive, less explicit way. A picture, as the saying goes, can be worth a thousand words. We live in a world where people are continuously bombarded with messages and often make decisions in seconds, without taking the time to read even to the end of a single sentence. So remember the mantra 'Show, don't tell'.

AN IDENTITY IS A RECIPE
A visual identity is a collection of visual clues that you use to become recognisable. Your logo is just one of the ingredients: you have colours, fonts, styles of imagery, and compositional choices to work with. Combined in a particular way, they create a unique dish.

UNIQUENESS
The more unique your visual identity is, the easier it is to stand out from your competitors, and the easier it is to protect your brand legally.

CONSISTENCY AND DIVERSITY
You want to be as recognisable as you can, yet be able to communicate different messages to different audiences in different ways. A good identity helps you to be consistent, yet gives you the freedom to make every idea that you send out into the world surprising and different so that people can distinguish between them.

STAND OUT FROM THE CROWD

When you are part of a sector, a scene, or an industry that is traditionally not in the business of attracting one-on-one customers, it might seem that you don't need or want to have a differentiating brand. We often hear, 'But we are scientists, we have to look boring!' or 'We don't compete, therefore, we don't have to stand out.' But almost every organisation competes for something, be it a grant, a donor, press attention, or the favour of a government. Make sure you think carefully about who your audiences are and how they recognise you, before you decide whether a visual identity is important or not.

TEST YOUR FAVOURITE BRAND

Test your favourite brand by covering the logo on some of their materials. Which elements identify the sender of the message? The colour, the font, the tone of voice, the topic, the image style, the composition, or all of the above? The best brands in the world perform on many visual and verbal levels. What can you learn from this?

LOGO

The logo has come a long way from its origins as a marker of quality, ownership, and artistry. Often considered synonymous with branding, a logo is the flag under which an organisation sails, and also its most recognisable visual element. Its importance is often overstated, because no logo exists without a good set of other visual identity elements surrounding it. Still, an iconic logo can be a very valuable asset to a brand. About Coca-Cola, the most widely known brand name on the planet, it is often said that its brand and its logo are more valuable than the formula of the drink itself.

TRADEMARKING

Logos are often trademarked to protect a brand. Nike's logo, the swoosh, has been trademarked to such an extent that it is even forbidden to put up a building whose shape as seen in satellite images creates a swoosh. The trademarking process can help you not only protect your own interests, but also ensure that you are not infringing on another organisation's trademark. Changing a logo at a later date because of a lawsuit can be a serious loss of built-up brand recognition (not to mention extremely difficult and expensive).

CONTROVERSY

Nothing is as divisive as a logo! When a company publicly presents a new logo, it can create a wave of extreme reactions, both positive and negative. In 2014, the new Airbnb logo was mocked for looking like buttocks. A new Gap logo met with such ridicule that the company retracted it within three days. You can love a logo or hate it, but only time can tell whether it is a keeper. These days everyone seems to be a design critic. Designing visual identities is an expertise that cannot be underestimated, so make sure that you work with qualified professionals.

DYNAMIC LOGOS

With all the digital media and devices we have at our disposal, an identity no longer has to be a static form, with the same logo, colour and shape on each and every application. It can move, it can morph, it can tell an entire range of different stories.

IT TOOK ME A FEW SECONDS TO DRAW IT, BUT IT TOOK ME 34 YEARS TO LEARN HOW TO DRAW IT IN A FEW SECONDS —PAULA SCHER

CRITERIA

It's tough to judge whether a logo is right for you. Don't let your own tastes blind you. Ask yourself:
- » Is it unique and memorable?
- » Is it iconic? Are you tempted to redraw it yourself?
- » Is it timeless?
- » Is it scalable: what would it look like on the back
- » of an airplane's tail or on top of a ballpoint pen?
- » Can it be trademarked?
- » Can it be applied universally?

DON'T STOP AT THE LOGO

Even in the dark you can recognise a Coca-Cola bottle by its iconic shape. The minimalist style of Apple's product packaging and the care that goes into the materials does not even require the Apple logo; you can feel the brand's personality in everything the company produces. See a green and red painted building on the horizon in Kenya? You can bet your fortune that it's an MPESA facade.

VISUAL BRANDING TESTS
In the humanitarian sector there is no shortage of red logos with hands carefully cupping children, people in circles holding hands, or making seeds grow. In the business world, there is no shortage of globes and stripes and speed lines. Use the visual branding tests on page 195 to check whether you stand out from the crowd.

IT'S ALL
IN THE MOVEMENT!

The Uber screen starts out black with a tiny light dot that scales to a circle and back, reminiscent of a radar screen tracking a submarine.

MIT Media Lab looks at any challenge from a myriad of angles, which has been reflected in its scaling, shifting visual identity.

AOL is defined by a simple word mark that is placed on different backgrounds from cartoons to photorealistic flowers.

The USA Today dot changes content for each news category, from sports to foreign news to science.

THE STORY OF THE SWOOSH

In the history of branding, there are many legendary stories around logo decisions. Perhaps the most memorable is one about the Nike logo created by Carolyn Davidson in 1971 when she was a graphic design student at Portland State University. She met Phil Knight while he was teaching accounting classes, and she started doing some freelance work for his company, Blue Ribbon Sports (BRS). Over the course of a week, she presented half a dozen logo proposals. Knight was not convinced. He wanted something more iconic, like the three stripes used by Adidas, the main player in the market at the time. They ultimately selected the mark now known globally as the swoosh. 'I don't love it,' Knight told her, 'but I think it will grow on me.' The company paid her US$35 for her services. In September 1983, Knight gave Davidson a golden Swoosh ring with an embedded diamond, and an envelope filled with Nike stock to express his gratitude.

TYPOGRAPHY

A letter is the tiniest carrier of identity. A font has the power to give a face to personalities of every kind, from formal (serifs) to neutral (sans), from personal (scripts) to playful. Just as the shape of the glasses you wear says a lot about your personality, the shape of the letters you use can communicate a lot about your brand. Typefaces can be custom developed for a brand or chosen from one of the thousands of type collections in the world. Usually a brand identity uses one font for display purposes (big headers with lots of character) and another one for running text (to provide optimum readability at a small size). A standard system font may be chosen for use in word processing documents, in presentations or on websites.

Calibre Black

Lyon Display

CA script
custom developed for C&A

Franklin Gothic
Condensed

COLOUR

Even at the end of the world, atop the highest mountain, you will run into the ubiquitous shack painted in bright, Coca-Cola red. Ever since the Industrial Revolution brought us branding as we know it, colour has become a defining factor in branding. It is a powerful tool in the struggle to stake out your own territory. In every country and in every industry, certain colours are synonymous with certain brands. In the European mobile phone market, the magenta of T-Mobile battles the red of Vodafone, and the green of KPN. Many brands claim their colour within an industry because the recognisability it creates is so incredibly important to their ability to be recognised.
A set of colours can be just as iconic as a single colour.
By creating a palette of a particular colour combination, you can create richer expressions, or use different colours to label different products and services.

IMAGE CONCEPT

How can you create a rich expression beyond your logo? Some organisations bank on the clarity and simplicity of pictograms. Others want to show a more personal, individual personality through handmade illustrations. Sometimes the realism of a photo is the most expressive choice, and there are dozens of different photographic styles to choose from, the gritty realism of photojournalism, the drama of an artistic black-and-white shot, and the spontaneous fun of a snapshot, just to name a few. From selfies to skilful technical portraits, the way you use images says just as much about you as what you show with them. Find a style that fits your personality and the story that you are trying to tell.

YOU CAN'T BE
WHAT YOU CAN'T SEE

A huge part of the visual imagery that brands use to tell their stories is photography. Much of the imagery we see daily portrays a familiar trope: men leading, women sidelined or sexualised, and mum and dad in stereotypical roles. The Lean In Foundation (founded by Sheryl Sandberg) is trying to shift that paradigm and realised that one way to do it is to literally make the shift visible. LeanIn.Org and Getty Images have teamed up to create the Lean In Collection: a library of thousands of creative images devoted to the powerful depiction of women and girls, families of all kinds, and men as caretakers. Their photography can now help brands tell the right stories.

MANAGING YOUR IDENTITY

A verbal and visual identity are combined in all brand expressions, from campaigns, to events, to HTML newsletters, and often these expressions are developed by different experts. To make consistent implementation easier, a brand book with the brand's guiding principles can be developed, with specific inspiration and guidelines on the use of the visual and verbal identity. A starter kit with a logo set for print (CMYK) and screen (RGB), Adobe colour palette and standard files of other identity elements ensures that everyone implementing your brand identity works from the same foundation, avoiding colour differences, placement mistakes and making the implementation process more efficient.

LAYOUT PRINCIPLES

An often overlooked way to distinguish your messages is by using a unique layout or composition principle. A French warehouse places its red square logo in the centre of every message it produces, from newspaper advertisements to billboards in the Paris subway. The not-for-profit 'Igniting Change' uses bold messages in type as its main layout feature. It highlights parts of stigmatising words that reveal a more positive angle ('elderly' becomes 'elder', 'prisoner' becomes 'son'). Spotify, the music streaming app, was looking for a visual identity that embodied the spirit and emotion of music. The initial brand identity created early on worked for the app but not for an emotional brand experience. Their brand agency Collins created a visual language of colors and shapes that could create a myriad of layouts to overlay on top of the existing artwork of artists' albums. To manage the creation of hundreds of thousands of images, they created a piece of software for Spotify s employees to easily create Spotify branded artwork.

Brand Interactions

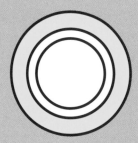

A brand is only as strong as the meaningful ways in which you bring it to life. How does your inner core express itself in experiences that build your brand with your audience? Talking with one of your team members, using your service, seeing you speak at a conference, and reading your tweets are all just some of the ways that people form impressions of you, experiences that shape how people think and feel about you. Interactions with your audience are where people will discover whether you walk the walk or just talk the talk.

WHAT IT ENCOMPASSES

- Communication and channels.
- People, talent and behaviour.
- Places and events.
- Products and services.
- Production line and sourcing.
- Partnerships and collaborations.
- Technology.

WHAT IT'S FOR

- Directing how people think and feel about you through their interactions with you.
- Translating your inner character, beliefs and personality into tangible experiences.
- Creating surprising yet consistent experiences across all your interactions.

COMMUNICATION & CHANNELS

There is no shortage of ways to communicate: digital or print, spoken or written, in a year-long campaign or a 30-second video, through billboards or social media. The general trend is towards conversation and content, and away from the one-way messages of traditional advertising.

Your communication can be divided into several categories
» Internal communications (team, investors, board members)
» External communications (ongoing: updates, opinions, events invitations, etc. building brand recognition)
» Campaigns (concentrated efforts on a particular topic or event)

In the age of social media, everyone is opening accounts and shouting at the world, hoping for their messages to get to the right people, or their videos to go viral. This only happens to a very small fraction of people and organisations, and is often the result not of a strategic intent but a serendipitous stroke of luck. The road to hell is paved with campaigns that were not retweeted and videos that never made it past 200 views.

Given all the options you have, it is even more important to work from your brand core and to brainstorm about which communication and channels fit your personality and your purposes. Key to any good communication strategy is understanding your audiences, what their concerns are, what you offer as a gain, where they hang out (physically and digitally) and what information needs they have, so you can start a conversation. Every audience segment has a channel that offers you the best return on your energy.

Communications can really become a purpose on their own. You can get too focused on things that don't move the dial. When you are just starting out it can be really hard to measure the success of communications because you don't yet know what the benchmark should be for success. Two thousand likes on a post is great, but not if it doesn't convert to action. Getting press coverage is fantastic, unless it is on a platform your audience does not frequent. Make sure you work strategically. Set a goal, create a hypothetical communications approach, launch it small, test the impact, improve and try again.

CUSTOMERS ARE NOT THE ONLY AUDIENCE

When you think about developing interactions with audiences make sure you don't only think about customers, users or clients! You have many audiences that you need to reach like present or potential partners, employees, investors, suppliers and the press!

CHANNELS
Check out the 19 channels you have at your disposal on page 155.

REACHING THE PROFESSIONAL COMMUNITY

Business services and individuals looking to build a personal brand around their expertise can look at LinkedIn groups and updates, do a TED Talk, publish newsletters, or use blogging platforms like Medium or SlideShare. Still, a personal email introduction or phone call to your new client might have more impact than a thousand tweets. A 30-minute presentation at a fair or conference might expose you to more potential talent for your team than an employment advert. Almost every industry has a magazine or platform where you 'need to be seen', for example the *Stanford Social Innovation Review* for entrepreneurs in social impact, or *Mongabay's Wildtech* for the best source of thinkers around tech for wildlife. Decide where you need to be seen so you can find a way to make it happen.

REACHING OUT TO INDIVIDUALS

Organisations reaching out to 'consumers' operate in a very different and very crowded space. A Kickstarter campaign can get you more fans than a year of posting on Facebook. Again, the question to ask is where your crowd hangs out. A pop-up shop in a neighbourhood can help you build a closer relationship with people than a mere digital presence can. Yoni, the organic sanitary brand from Holland, started out with personal promotion outside the bathrooms of clubs and cafés.

MAKE IT CURRENT

Communication should never exist for the sake of communication. Communication happens as a result of other brand interactions, through the events you organise, such as a dinner for potential investors, a hackathon for social good, the launch of a new flavour of chocolate bar, or the release of your annual report. Smart entrepreneurs plan ahead and see opportunities to make the most of each interaction. You could even organise an event to create a current edge to your communication that will be timely for others to share and build on.

SHARING CONTENT

In the fight to attract people's online attention, creating content is the way many brands build their story and personality. In March of 2014, Lush featured the story of the hen harrier (a bird on the verge of extinction, with only six adults left alive in the world) on its homepage as a full feature. The story was completely unconnected to their products, but very much connected to their environmental values. A brand that uses so much space on their biggest sales channel to talk about things that truly matter to them builds a lot of love with audiences.

To establish thought leadership in a particular area, experts share their ideas and knowledge with the world. By showing your expertise, you direct what you want people to recognise you for. Whether it is through blogging, a TED Talk, a book or quotes over Twitter, ideas and knowledge are a valuable commodity.

CREATE CONTENT THAT IS TRULY WORTH SHARING

But content only works when it is truly valuable to your audience. Content is a very crowded space. If you do want to go forward with content creation and curation, track the hours you are investing in it and the cost. Measure it against, for instance, paid social ads.

PUT YOUR AUDIENCE IN THE SPOTLIGHT

Brands that put their fans and customers in the spotlight receive a lot of love in return. Sugru, the mouldable rubber, encourages customers to submit photos of their creations and publishes them as an inspiration for others. THNK, the School of Creative Leadership, is a great platform for participants, who are featured heavily on the website, on campus and in company communications. These kinds of interactions build up a rich set of signals and impressions in the mind of your audience and help to create loyalty, preference and, hopefully, the enthusiasm to tell others about you.

SUGRU
Read the case study about Sugru on page 53 to learn more about their engagement with users.

PEOPLE, TALENT & BEHAVIOUR

Who are the people that are the face of your organisation? How do they behave? What type of talent do you want to attract? Engagements with the people that make up your brand are the experiences that will tell your audiences what you are truly all about.

If every member on your team is aligned with what you do and why that matters, you can create experiences that leave a lasting impression. Whether it is a phone conversation, a keynote presentation, or everyday delivery of services, these points of contact have the potential to create the biggest impact on what people think and feel about you.

YOUR HR POLICY CAN BE THE STRONGEST FORCE IN BRINGING YOUR BRAND TO LIFE

But it's not just about your external audiences. What you have defined in your brand core should also guide how you select and reward the people you surround yourself with.

CHIPOTLE: STORIES WITHOUT WORDS

Mexican slow-food-served-fast chain Chipotle has been on the rise in the past decade, steadily growing their fan base. The restaurant brand has been successful in catching the wave of increased awareness around fast food, nutrition and ethics, and can even be credited with contributing to that wave's momentum. They tell the story of redesigning the food industry using heartwarming and endearing animations in which farmers and scarecrows look at the industrial food complex and decide to go back to real farming and real food preparation. The videos share an emotional, easy-to-grasp, hard-to-disagree-with manifesto, without using a single word.

REI: DON'T COME TO OUR STORE

On the occasion of Black Friday, the busiest shopping day in the USA, outdoor gear retailer and co-op REI launched the campaign #OptOut announcing that they would be closed on Black Friday and encouraging everyone to go and enjoy the outdoors that day. Fans of the store shared over 40,000 tweets and massive media coverage followed.

SURF'S UP AT PATAGONIA
When you walk into the Patagonia headquarters in California, the first thing that greets you is a chart with the surf conditions. Employees are constantly encouraged to go out and enjoy the waves, even if it's during work hours.

PLACES & EVENTS

Translating outwards from your brand's core, where do you want to be seen? How will you bring people together? In what places do you belong? What does your space look like? The physical context in which you operate can say a lot about who you are and what you do, influencing the impressions and experiences of both the people inside your organisation and outside it as well.

Significant places can be the location, type and design of your workspaces, entire buildings, geographical locations (a village, city, region, country or continent) or even virtual hangouts, that are intertwined with your sense of self.

The same goes for events. Where can your audience encounter you in a way that adds to their understanding of you? Do you need to be seen at TEDxEducation, SXSW or at Design Indaba? Where is the biggest concentration of the people that you need to reach? Make sure you are there!

Or will you create your own events?

Screaming about your brand from the rooftops in the hope that people and press will simply pick up on it is naive. Journalists need urgency, a moment, to feature you: that makes you news. What better way to create a moment than to organise an event?

Events do not need to be a gathering of people in a physical location. Online hangouts, forums and events can attract large tribes of like-minded people.

AWESOME EVENTS

Designathon Works teaches children to think like designers and solve pressing global challenges using new technologies. They showcase their method in a one-day global event in Mumbai, Nairobi, Dublin, Amsterdam and Rio. The children and their inventions are the best brand ambassadors one could wish for, and *Fast Company* featured the first edition of the event on their front page.

Operating on the belief that a pair of jeans should be worn for as long as possible, jeans label K.O.I. implements a 'Triple-R' philosophy: recycle, repair, reuse. Customers are given special K.O.I. repair kits and pop-up events are hosted for in-person repairing parties.

Little Lotus Boutique hosts the #ethicalhour on Twitter. During this one hour on Monday evening, thousands of entrepreneurs discuss their challenges and lessons learned in building their ethical business.

Internet of Elephants organises public Hackathons and Datadives where wildlife enthusiasts, conservationists, wildlife lovers and techies come together to create innovative ideas for tech for wildlife.

Tony's Chocolonely organises Tony's Talks where anyone can come to their headquarters for an informal talk on a new chocolate bar or development, have a beer and, of course, chocolate.

PRODUCTS & SERVICES

Your products and/or services are the most direct ways in which you interact with your audience. Some organisations are entirely based around a single product, while others have a menu of dozens of complex business services. The first priority of all brand development should be to ensure that your actual product or service delivers on its promises and, if possible, exceeds them.

Check if all elements of your brand core are represented in the products or services you deliver. Check if the identity is applied to them in the most effective way, and research whether the delivery of the product or service aligns with who you are.

Translating a strong brand core to a set of products and services can help to reverse engineer great new ideas! Looking at your brand core, which services and products do you deliver? What is your current 'menu' of offerings? And, given your newly defined brand core, what else could you offer? Think it forward and use your brand as a tool to create potential new business ideas. Ideate products and services from your brand essence that you might have never considered.

PARTNERSHIPS & COLLABORATION

The kind of company you keep is probably the most telling indicator of your intentions, and partnerships are best built when people share visions, values and audiences, or when they have complementary offerings. Clearly framing who you are, what you do, and why it matters allows you to find partners more easily.

A shared view of the world helps you to create a strong connection with impact investors or funds. A shared mission can be a great base for a collaboration with another organisation in the same area of interest. Shared values can forge a lasting relationship with a supplier or producer. Sharing an audience with similar characteristics can be a great way to cross-promote the services of two complementary organisations. One and one is three!

KIVA AND TRIPADVISOR: A LOVE STORY

The partnership between Kiva and TripAdvisor is a match made in heaven. The donors of the peer-to-peer microfinancing platform Kiva, and the travellers that review activities, hotels and cultural sites on TripAdvisor, are often global citizens looking for closer connections with people in other cultures. They are open to and supportive of local economic development. TripAdvisor reaches out to people travelling to a Kiva-supported country who wrote a review for that trip on their site. They then invite these travellers to choose a borrower in the country they visited to receive a $25 microloan on Kiva.org. The loans are entirely funded through a $250,000 contribution from TripAdvisor and come at no cost to the traveller.

TECHNOLOGY

Technology offers an unlimited number of possibilities to create closer relationships with your audiences and to make them fans of your venture.

What are the tools you use to do what you do? Is there an opportunity to develop new tech tools of your own based on your mission? Is there a way that tech can help you to visualise a future that you are striving for, or to make the past come alive? Technology offers enormous possibilities to create closer relationships with your audiences and to make them fans of your venture.

For instance THNK, the School for Creative Leadership, held a 'Taste of THNK' event, where government officials, investors and other important guests would receive updates on the school's progress since its funding. Simple applications of technology were used to surprise guests. At the reception desk, they received a name badge containing a hidden RFID chip. To their surprise, when guests entered the space, their names appeared on a large screen onstage welcoming them to the event.

NEW OPPORTUNITIES

Love Matters uses a WhatsApp broadcasting list to share sexual health reproduction and rights information with subscribers in India.

Internet of Elephants uses data and Augmented Reality to connect people to individual wild animals and conservation projects.

EXAMPLE: LUSH
BRINGING BRAND ANATOMY TO LIFE

A strong brand isn't made by listing values on a website or slapping a logo onto products. The magic of a strong brand happens when you manage to weave all of a brand's myriad parts into a cohesive whole with its own unique quirks, characteristics and personality. The UK body care company Lush is very successful in coordinating all the parts of its brand anatomy to work together to maximum effect.

THE BRAND THINKING CANVAS
This tool on pages 168-171 will help you build a holistic brand from the core, to the identity and the expressions.

Despite working in a sector generally regarded as indifferent to animal rights and environmental protection, Lush has been able to translate the original founders' personal vision into a brand that operates from 850 stores worldwide.

BRAND CORE: FRESH, PRINCIPLED, INNOVATIVE
At the essence of Lush is one short statement, 'Life is fresh', expressed in fresh ingredients, fresh inventions and fresh campaigns. At its core, Lush is a campaigning company. They believe in standing up for animal rights, protecting the environment and supporting humanitarian causes. With hundreds of stores worldwide, they have a unique platform for their messages. The boldness of their activism against water pollution, nuclear weapons, animal testing or the breeding of animals for fur stands side by side with colourful, optimistic and bubbly products, imagery, messages and employees. Their brand promises are featured prominently on all their media: fighting animal testing, freshest cosmetics online, ethical buying, 100% vegetarian, handmade and naked packaging.

LUSH WEARS ITS PROMISES ON ITS SLEEVE, POSTING THEM PROMINENTLY AT THE BOTTOM OF EACH WEB PAGE AND FEATURING THEM IN EVERY STORE.

BRAND IDENTITY: BOLD AND BUBBLY
The name Lush came out of a customer competition, and its connotations of being fresh, green and abundant fit the company like a glove. Their campaigning personality shines through in their bold identity: black and white combine with large, handwritten chalk typography. The black-and-white type is used on protest signs and price signs alike. It's all about contrast: for every bold outspoken word or shape there is a bubbly, colourful, optimistic photo or sentence. Lush is made for visual communication: the scent and texture of their products

cannot be transferred to photography, but their colourful, bubbly, muddy and glittery aspects can: hands dripping in green mud, fingers soaking in pink and blue bubbles and chunks of buttery soap on a stack. Like modern food photography, the images feature Lush products tossed, broken and re-arranged for the most mouthwatering effect. Their campaigns for animal rights or against nuclear arms are equally visual, for example employees have dressed up like foxes in cages and posed in the shop window to protest hunting practices.

BRAND INTERACTIONS: PAMPERING MADE MEANINGFUL
Lush is a master at translating its brand into a thousand different surprising experiences for its customers.

Communication - Its print magazine, *Lush Times*, which is freely available in stores, combines stories about product origins, coverage of recent campaigns by Lush employees, and a catalogue of products, creating a triple assault on your heartstrings. Lush is constantly creating content around its products, people and causes. During one day in June, the homepage of the Lush website showed the story of the hen harrier, a bird on the verge of extinction, with only seven of the species left in the UK. Very few commercial brands would risk dedicating their main shopping channel to a bird, but this demonstration of Lush's commitment to its core values resonated with its customers.

Products - Because the Lush founders were conscious of how their products and business practices interacted with the environment, they were challenged to create entirely new products that could exist without packaging, reigniting sales of bar soaps and solid shampoos. Their values directly influence product innovation. The Lush Charity Pot is a hand and body lotion of which 100% of the purchase price goes to environmental, humanitarian and animal rights charities. In the first five years, customers donated two million dollars to charities through the Charity Pot programme.

Partnerships - Lush builds successful partnerships with organisations like Climate Revolution (founded by fashion designer Vivienne Westwood) by offering a design scarf as

a re-usable gift wrapping material, and with Shark Savers, for whom a special soap was created to raise awareness of shark finning, a brutal practice that kills 100 million sharks every year. Places and Events - The Lush shops engage your eyes, your nose and your hands. You can smell a Lush shop from around the corner. Lush uses food-presentation techniques to display its products: soap bars, for example, are stacked up like mouthwatering pastries. Chalkboards are used, reminiscent of greengrocers. As a shopper you get the impression the products are so fresh and natural that you could eat them. At the same time, the physical locations are used as literal billboards to broadcast the company's principles, and as the HQs for local campaigns. Online, you can find Lush Kitchen, where small batches of exclusive products are made fresh by hand every day, and no two days are the same.

Ethics Campaigns - Lush literally stands on a soapbox to draw attention to environmental, animal or humanitarian issues. For the Go Naked campaign to promote positive body imagery, Lush employees stripped bare, and the campaign posters were put directly in the shop windows, getting Lush into trouble with local decency laws across the world.

The Lush Prize - Lush decided to put its money where their its mouth is and founded the LUSH Prize, awarded annually for the best innovation in alternative product testing. The £250,000 prize fund focuses on alternatives to animal testing of medicines and beauty products. It is a way that everyone at LUSH, the customers, and the wider public can become involved in the fight to end animal testing.

Channels - With 943,000 likes on Facebook, 131,000 followers on Twitter, 124,000 on Instagram, 9,600 on Pinterest, Lush is a company fully committed to digital communication with its audiences.

Lush has thrived on building a holistic brand that unites pampering with principles and creating the ultimate synergy between actions and communications. People pick up on smaller and larger parts of its story at every point they come into contact with the brand, winning their preference and loyalty.

CHAPTER 4
BUILD YOUR BRAND STEP BY STEP

THE PROCESS

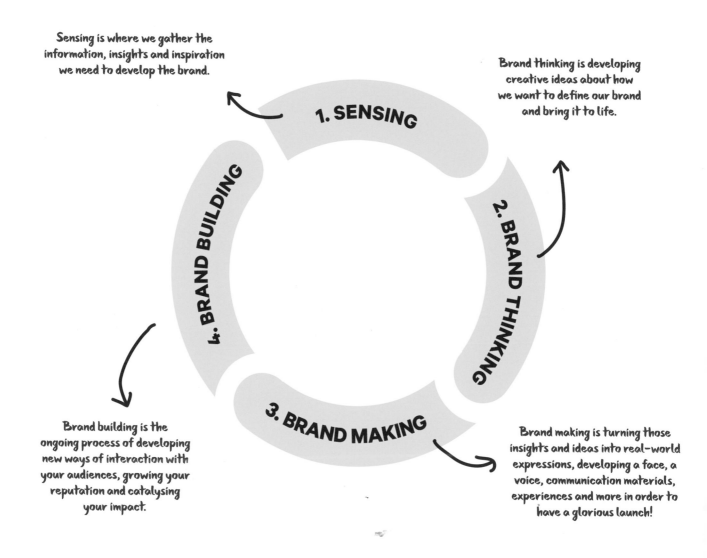

Sensing is where we gather the information, insights and inspiration we need to develop the brand.

Brand thinking is developing creative ideas about how we want to define our brand and bring it to life.

1. SENSING

4. BRAND BUILDING

2. BRAND THINKING

3. BRAND MAKING

Brand building is the ongoing process of developing new ways of interaction with your audiences, growing your reputation and catalysing your impact.

Brand making is turning those insights and ideas into real-world expressions, developing a face, a voice, communication materials, experiences and more in order to have a glorious launch!

If you feel branding is creating a logo and a website, you will see branding as a short, linear process. If you define branding as directing what people think and feel about you, it is an ongoing process that needs constant inspiration, investment and attention in order to help support your goals. The second view of branding provides you with the most positive effects over time. Through the brand development process, people and organisations go from being self-aware, to being self-defined, to having a self-directed brand.

We've outlined the brand development process in this chapter from A to Z. There is not one way to develop a brand. Different products, services, persons or ideas require their own routes to brand success. We have created an outline of the brand development process that covers the basics for a broad range of changemakers. It is not intended to be dogmatic: it is simply a guideline that you can use and adapt according to your own needs. Some of the steps have corresponding tools and exercises. Find empty tool templates to use for your own brand in the tool templates chapter.

PHASE 1
SENSING

In the sensing phase you do your homework. You explore the world in which your brand will be rooted. The more you know, the stronger the foundation for success.

1. CAPTURE YOUR INSIGHT
You have a big *aha* moment: an insight you think is the key to change. Define the insight, test it, hone it.

2. DEFINE YOUR BRAND PROPOSITION
What is it that your brand offers?
What is your proposal?

3. DIVE INTO THE WORLD OF YOUR AUDIENCE
Who is your primary audience and what drives them? Do the work to see if your proposition resonates with your audience and get to know their world.

4. MAP OUT YOUR MARKET
Based on your proposition, what is the market that you will operate in? Map out what the field looks like and where you want to be positioned.

5. ANALYSE THE COMPETITION
Understand who you compete with in order to build a brand that is unique and different from all the rest.

6. RESERVE RESOURCES
What will the branding process look like time- and money-wise? How will you budget for it? This is the moment to crunch the numbers.

7. GET SUPPORT
Unless you are a one (wo)man show, make sure that you have the support of your team for the branding process. Co-create where possible.

STEP 1
CAPTURE YOUR INSIGHT

If you are using this toolkit, at some point in the past few months or years, you have had a big insight. You've observed a problem or opportunity in the world and a need that people have that is not being met. This is what we call an insight. It is the foundation of your brand.

A strong brand starts with a compelling insight. It is the 'why' behind your product or service and dictates your position in the market. There are insights on many levels. Insights can lead to very innovative products and services; they can even lead to the creation of an entirely new market.

"The chocolate industry is built on slavery and unfair economic systems. As a chocolate addict I hate that I am contributing to slavery. I wish there was a chocolate bar I could eat in the knowledge that it is slave free and provides a good source of income for everyone involved."

"We've got a lot of complex problems to solve in the world but we are not educating people in how to solve them effectively. We need trained experts in social innovation."

Or, an insight merely serves as a new way to sell an existing product. Omo, a detergent company that has existed for 60 years discovered that parents value their kids getting dirty during play. Getting dirty means that the children have a chance to roam free, explore, play and learn. Therefore Omo developed a campaign around the insight: 'dirt is good'.

You often don't start building your brand directly after having your insight. Therefore, you will have to go back to your early thought process later on to identify what your big 'aha' moment was. Reimagine the problem you would have seen in the world and the need that is not being met to frame your insight.

DOES IT RESONATE?

Sometimes we are so in love with our insight for change that we forget to check if it resonates with our audiences. If your insight does not resonate, you are setting yourself up for failure. Make sure to test it, test it, test it, before you build your entire brand on an assumption.

INNOVATIVE

↑

New market — Amani Institute (training professionals for the social sector)
SpaceX (space travel for all)

New product
(or variant) — Sugru (mouldable glue)
BRCK (self-powered rugged Internet device for Africa)

New differentiator — Macmillan (cancer support)
Soko (fast fair fashionable jewellery)
Fresh Life (high quality public toilets)

New brand — Yoni (organic tampons)
Tony's Chocolonely

New way of
advertising — Omo (laundry detergent, launched campaign 'dirt is good')

↓

TACTICAL

SPOT THE INSIGHT
Brand insights are all around us.
Exercise your insight radar! See
page 165.

TOOL
INSIGHT
GENERATOR

You have an insight into how change can be created. You've made an observation, you see a dilemma people are struggling with. There is an unmet need that you can provide. This insight will drive your brand.

WHAT IT'S FOR

» Defining the insight that drives your brand.

HOW TO USE IT

» Express your insight as observation, dilemma, need.
» Start at your observation and work downwards.
» Capture your insight in one phrase that will become the foundation for your next steps.
» Test it with your audiences. Does it resonate with them? Do they recognise the dilemma and the need? Does the way it is articulated appeal to them? Test your insight through a structured testing process with respondents or pitch it one-on-one.
» If needed, adapt and test again.

OBSERVATION
An observation or fact about a problem in the world which is recognisable for your audience.

DILEMMA
Something that stops people from doing or feeling the right thing.

NEED
Articulation of what can be done to improve the situation.

IN SHORT
Frame your insight in one compelling phrase.

TONY'S CHOCOLONELY	AMANI INSTITUTE	OPRAH WINFREY
"The chocolate industry is built on slavery and unfair economic systems."	"We've got a lot of complex problems to solve in the world."	"I'm not getting everything out of life. I sometimes feel lost and down."
"As a chocolate addict I hate that I am contributing to slavery."	"We are not educating people in how to solve them effectively."	"I'm busy and there are lots of demands on my time. Where do you start to live a better, meaningful life?"
"I wish there was a chocolate bar I could eat in the knowledge that it provides a fair income for everyone involved."	"We need to train experts in social change."	"I need an easy-to-access, entertaining source of wisdom and information on living a full life."
Eating chocolate should never leave a bad taste in my mouth.	Social change should be a profession and an expertise.	Everybody could use some inspiration to live a full, meaningful life.

STEP 2
DEFINE YOUR BRAND PROPOSITION

Your next step is defining what you offer the world as a product or service to address the need you have uncovered. Your proposition is your offer, as simple and convincing as possible. A proposition must be unique, clear, purposeful and valuable to your audience. Test it with your intended audience to gauge the response and adapt if needed.

PRACTICE MAKES PERFECT

As a changemaker you are often completely clear on 'why' you are doing what you do but you will find it hard to clarify the 'what'. Solutions for complex social and environmental change are often not defined in one minute. Practice makes perfect. Don't be shy to tell dozens of people about your offer. Each time you have to describe it, you will get a little closer to the right phrase.

TONY'S CHOCOLONELY

Eating chocolate should never leave a bad taste in my mouth.

Tony's Chocolonely makes great chocolate while fighting for a 100% slave free chocolate industry.

FRAME GAME
Find creative ways to describe your proposition. Play the frame game on page 192.

TOM'S SHOES

I'm looking for a pair of fun summer shoes.

We've got great shoes and for every pair you purchase, you help a person in need.

AMANI INSTITUTE

Social change should be a profession and an expertise.

Through our higher education model, we develop professionals who create social impact.

UBUNTU LAB

Our country would thrive if people could get past their prejudices.

Ubuntu Lab creates educational programmes that help people understand people.

DIVE INTO THE WORLD OF YOUR AUDIENCE

In order to make the change happen that you want to see in the world, you need to have a deep understanding of your audience. This is the time to dive into their world to understand who they are and what they need, what their life looks like, their pains and motivation. You cannot afford to build your product or service on assumptions, so put in the hours needed to confirm that your proposition truly matches your audience's needs. Bring your research together in one or more brand personas.

Make sure you build your brand on your understanding of your primary audience. Who is your primary audience, you may ask?

Many organisations have audiences other than a traditional customer or client. Perhaps you first need investors. Or you have a donor and a beneficiary. Or you need a partner in order to deliver your product to customers.

When we develop a brand, we focus primarily on the audience that is the most crucial to our existence.

OFTEN THIS IS THE PARTY THAT GENERATES YOUR INCOME/REVENUE

A jeans brand focuses on the customer, even though it might be selling to stores. A solar-powered light donated to children in developing countries needs to focus on consumers in high-income countries who buy one light so the company can give one away. An app to train health-care volunteers needs to brand itself for the NGOs who buy product licences, not the volunteers themselves.

In some cases, organisations have two crucial audiences. This is often the case for businesses with a platform model. For instance: a job platform for people with disabilities needs to cater to employers and job seekers. Airbnb needs hosts and guests. Uber needs drivers and riders. Amani Institute offers a Social Innovation Program to individual fellows and custom programmes for the social sector.

SELLING SUSTAINABILITY
Read more about understanding the drivers of consumers of sustainable products in the guest essay by Stella van Himbergen on page 208.

TOOL
PERSONA
TEMPLATE

A persona is a fictional profile that represents a brand audience. Developing a persona helps you to bring the audience to life.

WHAT IT'S FOR

» Clarifying your approach to and relationships with your audiences.

» Personalising your audiences and giving them a presence in your thinking and planning.

HOW TO USE IT

» Do research into the world of your primary audience. Interview them, go to where they hang out.

» Create a fictional persona for one or more people representative of the group.

» Keep it simple. Work with a maximum

» of three to five personas.

» Make them real and compelling. Avoid clichés. Use a photo (of someone you don't know) that fits the profile and brings the fictional persona to life.

NAME + AGE	Gazal Abedini, 31
LIVES IN	London
PRIVATE LIFE	Single, social life revolves around girlfriends, running, books, music and dating

PROFESSIONAL EXPERIENCE

Job title

Freelance writer

Organisation

Writes for Fast Company, WIRED, Yahoo & others

Other experiences (past jobs, volunteer work)

Course on coding for journalists
Tried to be an independent fiction writer

Educational background

BA in creative writing

ACTIVITY & BEHAVIOUR

Generation which...

is in and out of freelance jobs and works in highly competitive environments

His/her role model is...

Rob Walker, writer with brilliant column in the NY Times

A well-known emotion

Frustration at the pace of work and abstraction of working online

Geographical orientation

Combination of tech plus social good hubs from San Francisco to Nairobi & Mumbai

NEEDS

Pains

Stories of new tech applications are a dime a dozen. She wants to work on stories with purpose.

Gains

Our platform for solution journalism offers resources on how to write about social solutions that work.

Needs

A structured method to write solution- based stories, best practice examples

QUOTE

Something you would hear him/her say

'I want to be part of something relevant instead of churning out stories about new tech startups all day.'

SOCIAL & TECH

Tech literacy level

High! Can code and very familiar with online, interaction, devices. First adopter.

Hardware

Fairphone, Fitbit

Social media

Twitter, Reddit

INTERACTIONS

Places

Coffeeshop with wifi

Events

SXSW, coding Meetups for journalists

Communication channels

Email, WhatsApp, Facebook messenger Instagram for private use, Twitter for professional use Bigtime Dropbox user

MAP OUT YOUR MARKET & STAKE YOUR POSITION

You want to position yourself clearly, and differentiated from your competition. This process starts by mapping out the market where your audience looks for a solution to their need. Understanding what this market looks like, who your competitors are and where you position yourself is crucial to build recognition and preference with your audience. A strong positioning will be the anchor for your brand building efforts, making them more efficient and effective.

The first step to mapping out your market is understanding what the characteristics of the market in which you will be active are.

Your insight and proposition will give you clues to these characteristics. We use the polar opposites of these characteristics to create an axis. Getting the characteristics right is not an easy job, and you will most likely find yourself investigating several possibilities.

Take for example Macmillan Cancer Support. They were facing more pressure to stand out amongst a growing number of charities and were hard to distinguish from other cancer charities.

Or let's take Chipotle, a US-based ethical fast food chain, as an example. They want to be recognised as a fast, healthy and ethical option for our ready made meals. Their proposition is: 'food with integrity, served fast'. This leads us to position them on an axis of fast food to slow food, processed to organic.

EXAMPLE:
MACMILLAN CANCER SUPPORT

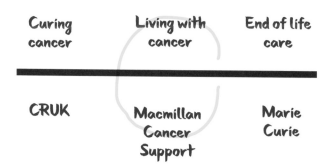

Curing cancer	Living with cancer	End of life care
CRUK	Macmillan Cancer Support	Marie Curie

EXAMPLE: CHIPOTLE

Proposition: Food with integrity, served fast.

Positioning

FAST FOOD

MacDonald's   Taco Bell

Chipotle

Burger King
Wendy's   Subway   Sweetgreen

Pizza Hut   Trader Joe's ready
                                             made meals
Local diners, snackbars

PROCESSED   **ORGANIC**

                                             Ottolenghi
Canned foods and tv   Local restaurants
dinners

                                             Ingredients from
                                             farmers markets

Home made meals   Grow my own
                                             veggies

SLOW FOOD

KNOW YOUR MARKET

It's vital you understand your market from your audience's point of view. As the only museum on human rights in your region you might feel you have a unique position in the museum landscape, but looking at your offer from the point of view of a potential museum visitor, you most likely will compete in a market of fun and informative family activities on a rainy Sunday afternoon.

FINDING A UNIQUE POSITIONING

When you look at your market, you will most likely find a lot of competitors positioning themselves on exactly the same spot. By redefining the characteristics of a market, you create new axes which in turn help you find an innovative approach which will make you stand out from the crowd. This can mean adding a new characteristic to an existing market, like THNK did (see the model on the top right). Or, by looking at the defining characteristics of your market you can find the exact opposites, as is the case with the law firm example on the bottom right.

DISCOVERING OPPORTUNITIES

Brand strategist Raquel Sztejnberg was working on the brand strategy of a law firm. While she was investigating the market, she realised all law firms present themselves as owners of knowledge with a traditional organisational model; 'the firm'. She found the polar opposite of the two and used them to create two axes: knowledge owners vs knowledge sharers on one hand, and the traditional firm model vs co-creative model. In the corner of knowledge sharers and co-creation, no law firm was yet active.

THNK, SCHOOL FOR CREATIVE LEADERSHIP
(market: innovation education)

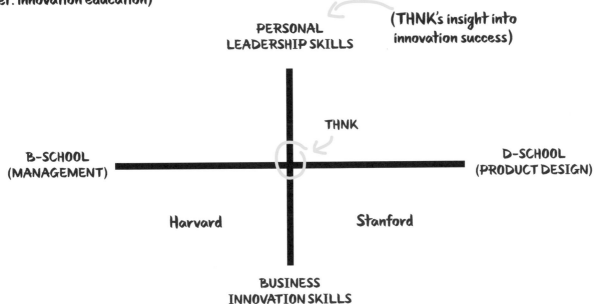

PERSONAL LEADERSHIP SKILLS

(THNK's insight into innovation success)

THNK

B-SCHOOL (MANAGEMENT)

D-SCHOOL (PRODUCT DESIGN)

Harvard

Stanford

BUSINESS INNOVATION SKILLS

LAW FIRM
(market: legal advice)

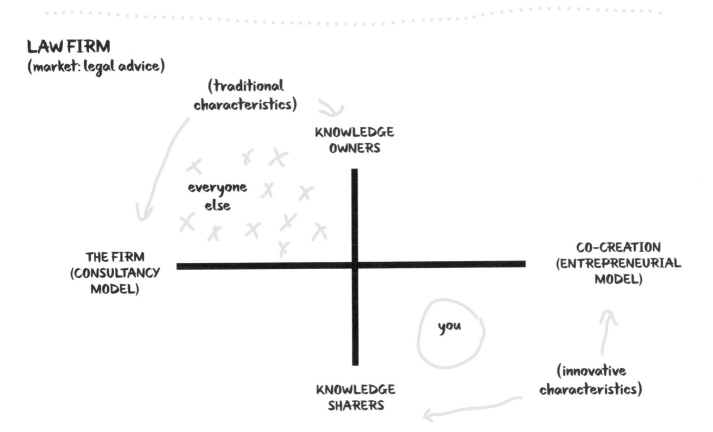

(traditional characteristics)

KNOWLEDGE OWNERS

everyone else

THE FIRM (CONSULTANCY MODEL)

CO-CREATION (ENTREPRENEURIAL MODEL)

you

(innovative characteristics)

KNOWLEDGE SHARERS

STEP 5
ANALYSE THE COMPETITION

Now that you have positioned yourself in the market, you know who your most direct competitors are. These are the people or organisations with whom you compete directly for clients/customers, investment or grants.

Dive into the world of your competitors. What do they look like, how do they speak, which channels do they use? What is the reason for the audience to believe they are the best choice? What works that you can learn from? What is something unique that no one else does that you can focus on? Create a brand analysis to find out. Apart from looking at competitors, you can also analyse a benchmark: a service, product or person that you think is a great example for the quality, look and feel or brand interactions that you aspire to. All this input will ensure you create a brand that is unique in the market.

A GREAT INVESTMENT

All the information on your market, positioning, and competition will come in extremely handy in the brand making phase as a briefing for your visual/verbal identity and later on when you start to create your first communications. See this work as an investment in the future.

COMPETITIVE ANALYSIS
Create a brand analysis of your most important competitors through this exercise on page 188.

RESERVE RESOURCES

Before you start the journey of developing your brand, make sure you have reserved the time and resources for the entire process and the maintenance throughout the year. Many organisations see branding and marketing as overheads. However, if we assume the product or service that you deliver is great, the one thing that stands in your way to growth is a lack of customers. Reserving resources ahead of time is a crucial step in the branding process.

WHEN YOU HAVE A STRONG BRAND, THERE IS NOT MUCH CONVINCING THAT NEEDS TO BE DONE —JULIE GREENBAUM, CO-FOUNDER AND CRO OF 'FUCK CANCER'

Most starting (social) entrepreneurs have little capital to invest in branding. It is not a question of how much budget to reserve: rather to conclude how much budget is available after all critical costs are covered. Whether we have a little or a lot, we need to understand what our budget can buy us and the consequences of the choices we make.

How much does brand development cost? The first step is to separate the cost of creating a brand from the cost of building it out over the years.

1
CREATING THE BRAND

Developing your brand is something you can do on your own or with your own team, up to a point. Unless you have copywriters or designers among your staff, or you are a talented web developer yourself, at some point you will have to invest funds into hiring people who have the skills you need to create advanced designs, strategies, messages, or communication materials. One of the most common questions people therefore have is, 'How much should branding cost?' Using housing as a simple metaphor can be very helpful in thinking about setting a budget.

IMAGINE BUILDING YOUR BRAND AS BUILDING A HOUSE

You can get a shack, an apartment or a villa. All three provide you with a roof over your head, but they are clearly different in price and what your money buys you. To give you an indication of what the investment range could be, see the table on the next page. The investments listed are merely an indication and differ widely from country to country. They are also influenced by three factors:

» What you get. Do you want a one-bedroom and a bus ticket to IKEA or a pre-furnished two-bedroom with state-of-the-art kitchen equipment?
» How much of your own time and skills you can invest. Do you buy the raw materials and build it yourself with a little help from a professional, or will you get it prefab and airlifted onto your plot?
» Who you hire. Do you get a young talent from your home town or a world-famous architect with a team of assistants?

When contracting work, always ask for a cost estimate with a detailed outline of deliverables. Most startups will start in the shack or the apartment and grow from there. If you are planning to grow, remember that your ability to add on to your house depends on the solidity of your foundation. If you choose not to trademark your name, or if the logo your nephew created can't compete in the big leagues, it can catch up with you later on. Forced rebrandings at a later stage can mean a loss of momentum, recognition, time and money.

2
BUILDING/MAINTAINING THE BRAND

These costs are usually captured in a marketing budget. You have to plan for two types of investments: time (of you, your team) and costs (external consultants, designers, materials, production cost, ad space etc.).

In founder teams, one founder usually needs to take on the responsibility of branding and marketing along with other activities. When the team grows to more than eight to ten people, a dedicated brand and communication role will be needed, with a potential support team over time.

Creating a budget for building and maintaining a brand is an art in itself about which a whole book can be written because of all the variables at stake. The budgets organisations reserve for their annual marketing can vary widely, from 5–50% of their annual revenue. The more competitive the market and the less personal interaction you have with your audiences, the more important marketing becomes and the higher the budget will need to be. For startups providing services directed at individual customers at a distance, such as apps or online shops, the branding and marketing percentage of resources will be considerable. For these digital products, experts recommend the following:

INVEST 50% OF YOUR TIME IN MAKING THE PRODUCT AND 50% IN GETTING TRACTION

Try to plan your marketing and branding expenses six months to one year ahead (build it into your investment plan or annual budget). Look at your calendar and project which costs you will need to make to create and support campaigns, events, collateral, ad space, consultancy and other third party costs.

BUDGETS IN THE REAL WORLD
In the Macmillan (page 44) and Soko (page 56) case studies, budget and return on investment are discussed.

		THE SHACK ↘
YOUR BUDGET		**1,000–5,000€** *a basic presence*
WHAT YOU GET	**Brand strategy**	
	Brand identity	• A designer to develop a rudimentary visual identity (logo, colours, type)
	Legal	
	Management and implementation	
	Communication	• A high-quality website template subscription like Squarespace • Styling of the template to fit your identity • Design of your basic communication materials such as a PowerPoint template, business cards, newsletter and social media branding
WHAT YOU HAVE TO DO YOURSELF		• Develop a brand strategy using DIY tools • Research competing and industry brands on the market • Test your offer with users/clients/customers • Brief and guide the designer/copywriter • Research name availability and claim your domain name and social media handles • Buy photo or illustration material or materials licensed for free use under Creative Commons • Implement your identity on communication materials and digital presentations • Generate ideas around brand building • Year-round promotions, social media, communications, PR, campaigns • Develop content for your site, blog or social media

THE APARTMENT *a professional presence*	THE VILLA *an ambitious presence*
10,000–25,000€	**25,000–150,000€**
• An independent brand developer or (small) agency to co-create, review or refine your brand strategy	• A brand agency creates your brand from scratch, and conducts competitive research and user research
• An independent brand developer or small agency to create a brand identity, including your name, messaging and visual identity (logo, colours, type, layout system, illustration or photography style) • Font licences to exclusive fonts	• Several brand identity concepts developed by the agency • Testing of the concepts with users if necessary • Optional: proprietary, custom-developed font
• A protected name trademarked in your primary market	• A protected name and logo trademarked in your primary and secondary markets
• A compact brand manual (PDF) with attached logoset and colour swatches that shows third parties how to apply the brand	• A brand manual (PDF) or portal with extensive examples and downloadable files that allow third parties to apply your brand more efficiently
• A professional website template customised to your needs • Design of basic communication materials, key infographics or models, important digital presentations (your TED Talk, pitch to investors) • A small set of visuals (photos, illustrations), either custom-developed or quality stock materials	• A storytelling coach to help you craft your story • A short inspiring/informative video • A professional website built just for your needs • All your communication materials developed by a copywriter and designer • A visual library of photography, iconography or video
• Develop a brand strategy using DIY tools like this toolkit, inviting the agency to join in the process • Brief and manage the creative process • Do market research and DIY testing • Claim your domain name for various extensions and social media handles • Develop content for your site, blog or social media • Generate ideas around brand building and implement them • Designate a person in charge of brand and communications • Craft your story or pitch and find platforms to test it • Year-round promotions, social media, communications, PR, campaigns	• Continually evolve your brand masterplan (using this toolkit) • Brief and manage the agency and your internal team • User testing and co-creation of concepts • Claim and maintain your domain name and social media handles + similar names • Build an internal team of brand ambassadors and give branding a seat on your board or management team • Manage social media • Develop content around your products/services

STEP 7
GET SUPPORT

When you invest time and resources into creating a brand, you need the support of your investors, board, co-founders and/or team. Each and every one of them will need to live your brand through what they do and say. Some of them will decide (with you) how much time and money can be invested in the process. This is the moment to speak to them about why you believe a brand is needed, what the branding process and decision making process will look like and how you plan on involving them.

CO-CREATE

A camel is a horse designed by committee, some people say.
And it is true that co-creating your entire brand with a large
group of decision makers can make the process difficult and
the results too much a compromise between many different
points of view. Still, creating certain parts of your brand in a
larger group can have great results because it creates early
buy-in and leverages the ideas of your team. Several tools
and exercises in this book are perfect for team work, such as:
the manifesto maker (co-create your manifesto with your
team), values game (choose and define your values together)
and the Brand Thinking Canvas (brainstorm brand interactions
with your team based on the core and identity).

PHASE 2
BRAND THINKING

In the brand thinking stage you create a blueprint for your brand.

1. DEFINE YOUR CORE
It is time to build the blueprint for your brand. We start at the core. What is the world that you are working towards? What are you doing to get there? Which values drive how you think and act? What are you committing to deliver?

2. BRAINSTORM YOUR IDENTITY
How will you translate the core to an outside identity? In what ways can you give your inner personality a face and a voice?

3. BRAINSTORM INTERACTIONS
Leverage your core and identity to bring your brand to life. Get creative with communication and channels, places and events, technology, making connections and more.

4. MAP OUT YOUR AUDIENCES
Based on the insight you want to be recognised for, which audiences do you need to reach, what do you want them to recognise you for and how will you get there?

5. PLAN FOR ACTION
Now that you have a mountain of ideas, it is time to look at the ones you will to put into action in the coming period so you don't lose them when it is time to build the brand. This is your brand strategy, the way in which you use your brand to achieve your goals.

STEP 1
DEFINE YOUR CORE

Now that you have done the required sensing, it is time to build the blueprint for your brand. We start at the core. Why do you do what you do? What does the world that you are working towards look like? What are you doing to get there? Which values drive how you think and act? What are you committing to deliver? The brand core drives your brand identity and all your actions and communications towards your audiences. It drives your organisational culture and the ethics you will base your decisions on.

TAKE YOUR TIME

When developing your own brand, it may seem logical to start at the centre of the model with the brand essence, but often the essence is the hardest to get right. Start with your vision, mission and values, and then find the most basic, compelling thread running through all of those elements: this is your essence. Sometimes, an ingenious phrase can pop into your mind. Or it takes a number of dedicated days or weeks to craft. Some people and organisations build a truly unique essence step by step over the years.

VISION VISUALISATION
Do you find it a challenge to create an exciting, unique vision? Jumpstart your brain by visualising it using the exercise on page 189.

TOOL
BRAND THINKING
CANVAS #1

The Brand Thinking Canvas represents the holistic anatomy of a strong brand. In this step of the brand development process we are going to look at the core, in yellow on the right.

WHAT IT'S FOR

» Defining the core of your brand; what it is that drives your identity and interactions.

HOW TO USE IT

» You create the brand blueprint based on the brand proposition for your primary audience.
» Work from the inside out but keep the brand essence for last.
» Start from the vision, mission, values, brand promises. End with the brand essence.
» Keep it short. If you start to see entire paragraphs or bullet lists appear on a sticky note, you are working in too much detail.
» If you have two primary audiences, your vision, mission and values should be unified under one brand and you create two sets of brand promises, one for each audience.

NEED A HAND?

Find tools to help you develop your mission and vision on the next pages.

EXAMPLE: MAMA CODE

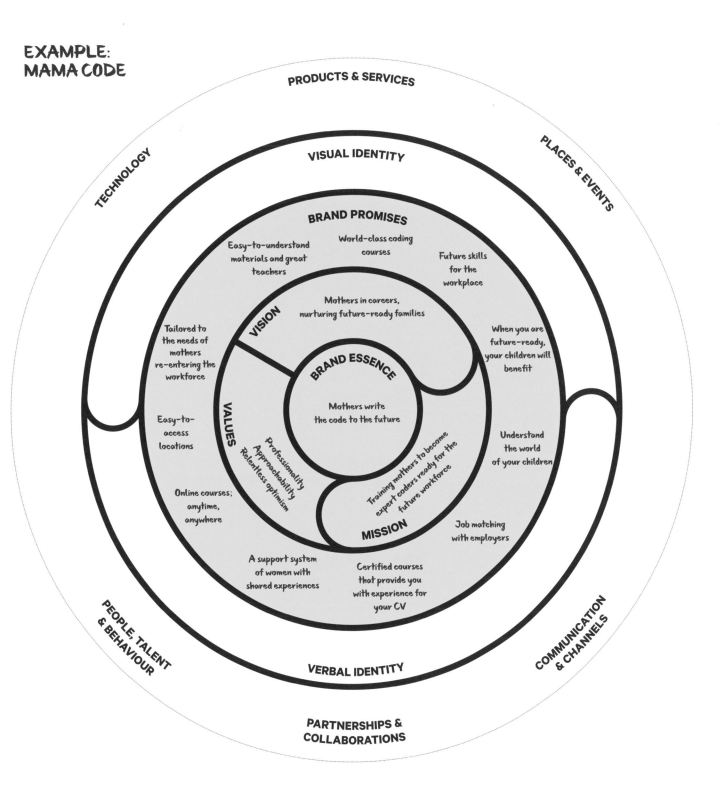

PRODUCTS & SERVICES

PLACES & EVENTS

TECHNOLOGY

VISUAL IDENTITY

BRAND PROMISES

Easy-to-understand materials and great teachers

World-class coding courses

Future skills for the workplace

VISION

Mothers in careers, nurturing future-ready families

BRAND ESSENCE

Mothers write the code to the future

Tailored to the needs of mothers re-entering the workforce

When you are future-ready, your children will benefit

Easy-to-access locations

VALUES

Professionality
Approachability
Relentless optimism

Understand the world of your children

Online courses; anytime, anywhere

Training mothers to become expert coders ready for the future workforce

Job matching with employers

MISSION

A support system of women with shared experiences

Certified courses that provide you with experience for your CV

PEOPLE, TALENT & BEHAVIOUR

VERBAL IDENTITY

COMMUNICATION & CHANNELS

PARTNERSHIPS & COLLABORATIONS

TOOL
THE CLIMB

Often people get their mission and vision confused. The Climb Tool helps you get it right.

WHAT IT'S FOR

» Defining your mission and vision.

HOW TO USE IT

» Start with your vision, the destination of your climb. What is the change that you want to see in the world?
» Make sure you formulate your vision as an end result. Make that end result as tangible and clear as possible.
» Work backwards from your vision towards your mission by defining how you will get to the top of the hill. By which means? Offering what type of value?

YOUR VISION

THE WORLD YOU WANT TO SEE

"I want to see a forest full of trees."

What does the world look like that you want to help create? What will the lives of your audience look like when you successfully deliver your product or service?

WAKA WAKA wants to see a world without energy poverty.

Nest is creating the thoughtful home: a home that takes care of the people inside it and the world around it.

ColorOfChange.org wants to see a United States where all Americans are represented, served and protected regardless of race or class.

SolarCity wants to see a world where renewable energy is cheaper than fossil fuels.

SpaceX wants to see 1 million people on Mars.

YOUR MISSION

WHAT YOU DO TO MAKE IT HAPPEN

"I am going to plant the seeds that make the trees grow."

What do you do and how does it contribute to realising your vision?

WAKA WAKA is a solar light that doubles as a device charger to enable people on the road or off the grid to have the energy and light they need to be productive.

ColorOfChange.org is strengthening Black America's political voice. Using the Internet, we keep our members informed and give them ways to act on pressing issues facing Black people in America.

Nest reinvents unloved but important products in our homes.

SolarCity designs, finances, and installs solar power systems that change the solar energy game to make it cheaper, greener and more accessible for everyone.

SpaceX revolutionises space technology, enabling people to live on other planets.

TOOL
MISSION COMPOSER

A mission statement is an effective way of getting your audiences to truly understand what you do, why you do it, and why it is important.

WHAT IT'S FOR
» Clarifying what you do, for whom and why.
» Galvanising support.

HOW TO USE IT
» Follow the arrows.
» Can't find the right words? Use thesaurus.com to find alternatives.
» Can't find the right sentence? Write each word on one sticky note to form a sentence and place alternatives beneath it.
» Summarise your mission in one short, compelling sentence.

WHAT IS THE PROBLEM YOU ARE ADDRESSING?

80% of blindness is avoidable. Existing eye-care tools are expensive, difficult to use and inaccessible. People don't get treated quickly enough, or at all.

SUMMARISE!

We are empowering health workers by providing portable tools to help detect avoidable blindness.

What is your mission in one short, compelling sentence?

WHO YOU ARE

This is where you come in!

We're Peek Vision! We're a team of technologists, eye specialists, public health doctors and product designers who are passionate about making high-quality eye care available to everyone.

WHAT YOU DO

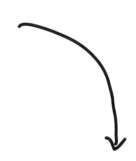

Peek Vision turns smartphones into comprehensive eye-exam tools. We develop easy-to-use eye-care tools for every clinic and health care worker.

The service(s) you provide.
The products you make.

WHY IT MATTERS

With our tools, health workers can detect, treat and cure preventable blindness on a large scale, helping people escape the challenges that blindness brings.

How you resolve the problem in the first circle.

TOOL
THE LADDER

When you are defining a brand promise for customers, the ladder helps you to move up from a functional promise (what) to an impactful promise (why) at three different levels.

WHAT IT'S FOR
» Easing into progressing from a functional promise to a more emotional value for your audiences.
» Brainstorm brand promises.

HOW TO USE IT
» Start at the bottom step and work your way up.

THE GRAND VISION
What the world looks like when the ultimate effect of the work has been reached.

Open minds are the foundation of a more peaceful and tolerant world.

SOCIETAL BENEFIT
Why it matters: what the world looks like when all users or beneficiaries are reached.

Knowing our family and ancestry brings us closer together and makes us feel part of a bigger picture. When we see how diverse our DNA is, it opens our minds to other people and other cultures.

AN EMOTIONAL PROMISE
Why it matters: what value it adds to people's lives.

Find out what your DNA says about you and your family. Contact your DNA relatives across continents or across the street. Build your family tree and enhance your experience with relatives.

A FUNCTIONAL PROMISE
What you do/what your product does.

We sell personal genetics test kits that help you find out more about your ancestry.

STEP 2
BRAINSTORM YOUR IDENTITY

Now is the moment to think about ways you can translate the core to a visual and verbal identity. Your face and your voice will be the consistent representations of your brand across all channels. Think of your identity as translating your brand personality into a logo, colours, imagery, name, tone of voice. What is the look and feel that perfectly translates what you are all about? Make it as unique and individual as you can.

✂ VISUAL AND VERBAL IDENTITY
An in-depth description of visual and verbal identity elements and examples can be found from page 74 onwards.

BRAND THINKING CANVAS #1

In this step of the brand development process we are going back to the Brand Thinking Canvas to look at the aspect of identity, in yellow on the right.

WHAT IT'S FOR
» Brainstorming your visual and verbal identity.

HOW TO USE IT
» Translate the core into a face and a voice. Based on the core, what is your name? How do you speak? What do you speak about?
» How do you see the core come to life visually? What colours represent it, what kind of typography, what do you show in photography, or do you use illustrations?
» Think of this aspect of the brand as the provider of personality. What kind of personality will your brand be?
» Create a moodboard if you love to work visually.

EXAMPLE: MAMA CODE

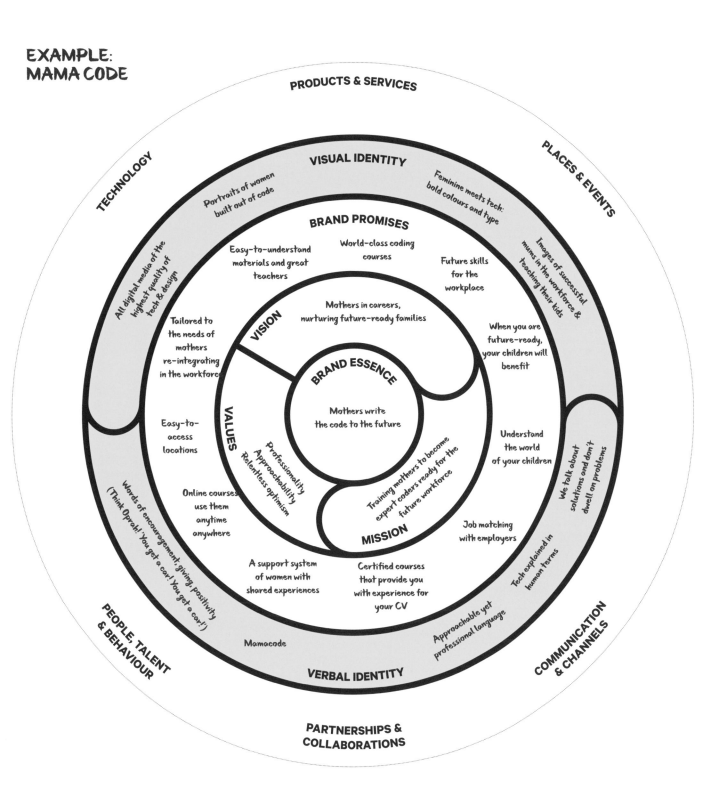

PRODUCTS & SERVICES

TECHNOLOGY

PLACES & EVENTS

VISUAL IDENTITY

Portraits of women built out of code

Feminine meets tech: bold colours and type

BRAND PROMISES

All digital media of the highest quality of tech & design

Easy-to-understand materials and great teachers

World-class coding courses

Future skills for the workplace

Images of successful mums in the workforce & teaching their kids

Tailored to the needs of mothers re-integrating in the workforce

VISION

Mothers in careers, nurturing future-ready families

When you are future-ready, your children will benefit

BRAND ESSENCE

Mothers write the code to the future

Easy-to-access locations

VALUES

Professionality
Approachability
Relentless optimism

Understand the world of your children

We talk about solutions and don't dwell on problems

Online courses use them anytime anywhere

Training mothers to become expert coders ready for the future workforce

Job matching with employers

Words of encouragement, giving, positivity (Think Oprah! You get a car! You get a car!)

MISSION

Tech explained in human terms

A support system of women with shared experiences

Certified courses that provide you with experience for your CV

Mamacode

Approachable yet professional language

PEOPLE, TALENT & BEHAVIOUR

VERBAL IDENTITY

COMMUNICATION & CHANNELS

PARTNERSHIPS & COLLABORATIONS

STEP 3
BRAINSTORM INTERACTIONS

This is the moment to brainstorm all the ways you can bring your brand to life! We've identified six ways in which you can create interactions with your brand audiences: channels and communications; products and services; people, talent and behaviour; technology; products and services; and events and places. This is the moment to think without constraint about all the ways in which you can translate your brand core into great interactions with audiences.

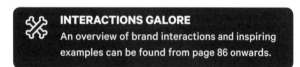

INTERACTIONS GALORE
An overview of brand interactions and inspiring examples can be found from page 86 onwards.

BRAND THINKING CANVAS #1

In this step of the brand development process we are going back to the Brand Thinking Canvas to look at the aspect of interactions, in yellow on the right.

WHAT IT'S FOR
» Brainstorming how your core is translated to interactions that give your audiences a clear idea of who you are and what you stand for.

HOW TO USE IT
» Start at any of the six types of experiences.
» Look at your core: how does it translate to what type of people you hire, what type of partners you want to be seen with, what type of events you attend or develop? etc.

EXAMPLE: MAMA CODE

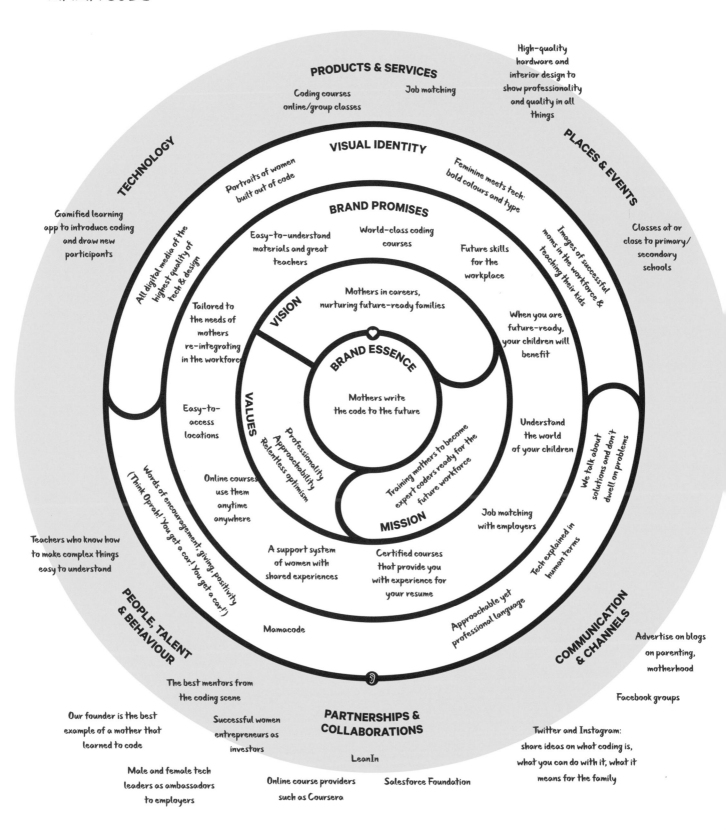

PRODUCTS & SERVICES

Coding courses online/group classes

Job matching

High-quality hardware and interior design to show professionality and quality in all things

TECHNOLOGY

VISUAL IDENTITY

PLACES & EVENTS

Gamified learning app to introduce coding and draw new participants

Portraits of women built out of code

Feminine meets tech: bold colours and type

Classes at or close to primary/ secondary schools

BRAND PROMISES

All digital media of the highest quality of tech & design

Easy-to-understand materials and great teachers

World-class coding courses

Future skills for the workplace

Images of successful moms in the workforce & teaching their kids

Tailored to the needs of mothers re-integrating in the workforce

VISION

Mothers in careers, nurturing future-ready families

When you are future-ready, your children will benefit

BRAND ESSENCE

Easy-to-access locations

Mothers write the code to the future

Understand the world of your children

VALUES

Professionality
Approachability
Relentless optimism

Online courses use them anytime anywhere

Training mothers to become expert coders ready for the future workforce

We talk about solutions and don't dwell on problems

Words of encouragement, giving positivity (Think Oprah! You get a car! You get a car!)

MISSION

Job matching with employers

Tech explained in human terms

Teachers who know how to make complex things easy to understand

A support system of women with shared experiences

Certified courses that provide you with experience for your resume

Approachable yet professional language

COMMUNICATION & CHANNELS

PEOPLE, TALENT & BEHAVIOUR

Mamacode

Advertise on blogs on parenting, motherhood

The best mentors from the coding scene

Facebook groups

Our founder is the best example of a mother that learned to code

Successful women entrepreneurs as investors

PARTNERSHIPS & COLLABORATIONS

Twitter and Instagram: share ideas on what coding is, what you can do with it, what it means for the family

LeanIn

Male and female tech leaders as ambassadors to employers

Online course providers such as Coursera

Salesforce Foundation

STEP 4
MAP OUT YOUR AUDIENCES

In order to realise your vision, you will need the support of more types of audiences than just your primary audience: investors, press partners, (potential) employees, beneficiaries, producers, etc. Understanding who these audiences are and mapping them out helps you to get a clearer understanding of how you can enlist them in your journey towards change. Defining what you want them to recognise you for and brainstorming how you can achieve that gives you a strategic roadmap for your actions and communications.

TOOL
GOAL
SETTING

Change never happens without the support of other people. By listing your goals you will uncover your brand audiences.

WHAT IT'S FOR

» Uncovering your brand's different audiences.

HOW TO USE IT

» Start with where you are now (Point A).
» List what defines your current situation.
» Think about a mid-term horizon of about three years as your future scenario (Point B).
» List what you would like to see as your future state. Don't just think about what is feasible: think about what is desirable.
» Make your answers specific and concrete.
» Identify the audiences that are needed to achieve your goals.

A   **WHERE YOU ARE NOW**

Cities are not designed by their citizens. Planners rule. We want to change this.

We are setting up an incubator for city changemaking entrepreneurs.

People know us, the two founders, but not our organisation (yet).

We have just received seed funding for the first six months.

We are a guy and a girl working two jobs.

We need to build a team of mentors, coaches.

We need to have a professional space, furniture and supplies.

B   **WHERE YOU WANT TO GO**

The mayor of Cairo has enforced the first two proposals coming out of our incubator.

    => city governments

The incubator is up and running with 16 in-house entrepreneurs.

    => primary audience: participants!

Our name is established in the region and starting to spread beyond.

    => press

We have successfully raised a new series of funding with impact investors.

    => investors

We are two founders with a supporting team.   => employees

We have ten international mentors, two coaches on call.

    => faculty

IKEA has sponsored our workspace and materials.   => suppliers

TOOL
BRAND THINKING
CANVAS #2

Part 2 of the Brand Thinking Canvas helps you map out your primary and secondary audiences and generate ideas on building the right brand recognition with them.

WHAT IT'S FOR
» Mapping out who your audiences are.
» Defining what you want them to think and feel about you.
» Brainstorming how you can achieve that.

HOW TO USE IT
» Copy your brand essence from the Brand Thinking Canvas part one.
» Map out the different audiences you need to make your product, services or idea a success.
» Start with your primary audience at the top and continue clockwise with the secondary audiences.
» First identify all the audiences, then dive into the what and the how per audience.
» First, define what you want them to recognise you for.
» Second, how will you achieve that recognition: through which actions and communications?

Game to introduce coding in a playful way, promoted through Facebook

Promotion at daycare centres, primary and secondary schools

Share facts & numbers: our percentage of participants who found a job after training

Booth at family festivals in summer

HOW
How will you achieve it? What are the key actions & communications?
Alumni who share their success stories.

AUDIENCE
POTENTIAL PARTICIPANTS
Audience segment and description

'Great opportunity to get my work life back on track with future-ready skills that make it easier to find a job.'
What do you want people to think and feel about you?

WHAT
'Hosting this group is a joy: great people, trustworthy, good cause! Make us look good too.'

WHAT
'Great place to fine-tune my craft and apply my knowledge for a good cause and meet potential employees.'

AUDIENCE
LOCATIONS (SPACE PROVIDERS)
Schools, educational institutes, cultural centres, libraries, coworking spaces

AUDIENCE
MENTORS & TEACHERS
Male & female techies between 21 and 40 with a passion for teaching

BRAND ESSENCE
Copy your brand essence from the Brand Thinking Canvas Part 1
Mothers write the code of the future

HOW
To attract: digital brochure with testimonials & photos. To charm: shout-outs & mentions in all our communications.

HOW
Speak at industry events and do a TED Talk. Use LinkedIn Groups to tell our story and get fans and supporters in the industry.

WHAT
'Great source of diverse and affordable talent for coding with dedication, passion and commitment.'

AUDIENCE
FUTURE EMPLOYERS
HR rep or founders of tech companies and traditional companies in transition

AUDIENCE
INVESTORS
Angel/social impact investors, Ministry of Labour subsidies, grants, Hivos, women's investment groups

WHAT
'This is a strong team with a sustainable, potentially profitable financial model plus great social impact. I want in.'

HOW
Showcase of our talent pool and participant projects online. Testimonials of other employers. LinkedIn + TED

HOW
Solid pitch deck and demo for pitch nights and events including our Business Model Canvas & impact numbers. List of founding investors on website

STEP 5
PLAN FOR ACTION

Now that you have created a blueprint for your brand, it is time to look at which actions you can take to make your brand a reality in the coming period.

REPUTATION TURNAROUND
Are you working on the brand of an existing organisation, product or service? Or your personal brand? And do you feel you have a reputation problem? People don't know what you do or stand for or have the wrong impression? Do the reputation turnaround exercise on page 196 to get your actions aligned with the reputation you want.

TOOL
ACTION PLANNER

Once you know what you need to do, don't let any of your insights slip away! Create an action plan that gives you an easy overview.

WHAT IT'S FOR

» Capturing what needs to be done in order to achieve your goals.
» Helping you get organised and ensuring that you put your thoughts into action.

HOW TO USE IT

» Fill it out after each major brand strategy session where you've come up with ideas on how to build your brand.
» Make it extremely specific and tangible.
» Update it continuously.

GOAL
What you want to achieve

Have a visual and verbal identity

Build a stronger company culture

Create focus in our profile

Get more people on board with our mission

Get better press coverage

ACTIONS What you will do to get there	RESOURCES Who & what you need to get it done	DEADLINE When should it be accomplished
Select a brand agency and review quotes	Write a brand brief	November 15th
Co-create a company manifesto with the team. Define our values and how we live them with the team	Set a date and block the calendar. Order food and drinks. Reserve main meeting room. Incorporate values into performance reviews.	January 4th
Update all descriptors on our website, Twitter, Facebook, Google search. Update LinkedIn profiles of the founders and employees.	Share unified mission statement with team and social media manager or digital agency and set an update deadline.	January 30th
Do a TED Talk.	Find out which TED platform offers the best match. Find out who is on the board of recommendation or find a former speaker who can introduce me. Write a short intro mail on why my idea is worth spreading.	March 12th
Reach out to Fast Company writer to pitch our story.	Get personal introduction through Mary Satiwa. Sit down with copywriter to craft pitch outline. Get great photos made at event. Create press page on website.	2nd quarter

PHASE 3
BRAND MAKING

In the brand making phase you will create the tangible assets that make up your brand.

1. CREATE A FACE AND A VOICE
Brand making involves the actual translation of ideas into tangible form, such as a visual and verbal identity.

2. MAKE SURE IT IS YOURS TO KEEP
Before going all the way, make sure your name and logo can be legally protected through a trademark and that you own your domain names and social media handles.

3. CREATE A BRAND BOOK
The identity is captured in a brand document that allows everyone who works with your brand to build consistent brand expressions.

4. CREATE FIRST EXPERIENCES
In the brand making phase you develop the basic experiences that are crucial to building the right brand with your audiences.

5. LAUNCH!
Choose a day to go public. It can be a big bang or a soft, gradual push, but on this one day, your brand will see the light.

STEP 1
CREATE A FACE AND A VOICE

It's time to create the face and voice of your brand, which are yours and yours alone. Your visual and verbal identity are going to be a very dominant factor in your life and work and will represent you to your audiences whenever you are not around personally. Needless to say, this step is not one to be taken lightly.

This is the stage of developing your brand where even the most hands-on entrepreneur needs to reach out to experts. You are going to look at your logo and write your organisation's name literally dozens of times a day, so you want it to be good.

WHO TO HIRE
Developing your verbal identity (name, tone of voice, editorial angle, messaging) and visual identity (logo, colours, type, imagery, layout) can be done by one party or several parties in collaboration. There is no right or wrong here: some people want to work with experts in a particular field so they will combine a dedicated namer with a designer who has a portfolio of projects that is exactly suited to your needs. Others want to have the assurance of one party taking on the entire job so there is a minimal risk of separate elements not being aligned. Depending on your preferred way of working, you can work with:

» A brand agency that develops your strategy, verbal and visual identity and creates your first communication items, or
» A consultant that develops your brand strategy
» A naming agency that develops your name and tone of voice and potentially your messaging, or
» A name consultant that focuses purely on your name, or
» A design agency or independent designer that develops your visual identity and potentially the ongoing communication items.

FINDING AN AGENCY

If you don't know any brand agencies, designers or namers already, it can be difficult to know where to start. If google is not giving you the results you want, try the following:

» What are brands you love and who has built them? Be bold, approach people and ask who is behind the work.
» Find the local or national association of designers or advertisers. They can refer you to agencies and sometimes even help you with your briefing
» If you are looking for designers: check out online portfolio sites like Behance or search Pinterest or Instagram.

WRITING A STRONG BRIEF

To ensure the experts you will work with are up to speed on what you are trying to achieve with your venture and with the branding process, you will need to write a brief. A good start is half the work. A well-written brief contains the right input and background information that you and your agency need for an effective creative process. The list on the right helps you to check if your agency brief is complete and creates a clear starting point that you can refer to at all phases of a project. You can use this brief to request estimates, for the start of the creative process and as a reference throughout.

CONSIDERING ESTIMATES

Take these points into consideration when you are reviewing estimates.

» When you ask several agencies to make an estimate for creative work, make sure you ask them all for the same deliverables or you will be comparing apples and oranges.
» Always ask, what is not included in this estimate? Legal checks, font licences, content development for a website and photography costs are regularly not included and can be a nasty surprise if you have not considered them ahead of time.
» Always ask, what is left for us to do at our end, based on this estimate? Do you need to do research, trademarking, domain registration yourself?
» If someone offers to do work for you at a discount or for free, check to see what this means for their deadline commitment and the legal ownership of the creative work once it is completed.

GUIDING THE PROCESS

If this is your first time guiding the development of a brand and creative agencies, it is important for you to have an overview of the entire process and know what success will look like. If it is possible to do workshops together to co-create strategic work and research, it can help both parties get off to a well-informed start. When reviewing creative work make sure you have pre-defined criteria for success. Of course, any concept that you choose should feel great and make you excited to get started. Some concepts can take some getting used to but really grow on you through time.

CREATIVITY DOES NOT EQUAL CHAOS

Creative thinking can go every which way and therefore it is crucial that the process which guides it stays the course. The goals and deliverables of the exercise should be clear, the criteria for success should be defined beforehand, and the decision making process (who has the final say, who gives feedback) in your team should be clear before you start.

CONSIDERING CREATIVE WORK
Are you presented with several creative concepts for a visual identity? Do the visual branding tests on page 195.

CREATIVE BRIEFING CHECKLIST

ABOUT THE TEAM

CLIENT — Who is the client and who wrote the brief?

CREATIVE — Who is this briefing for?
Is it an exclusive briefing or are multiple parties competing for the job?

PROJECT STAKEHOLDERS — Who is involved in the project?

MARKET & AUDIENCE

MARKET — What does your market look like? Where do you want to be positioned? Who is the competition? What makes you different?

AUDIENCE — Who are your audiences?
Can you share insights or background information?

COMM. & CHANNELS — Which existing communications and channels do you use to build relationships?

ON THE BRAND

INTRODUCTION — Who are you, what do you do and what are you trying to achieve? Use the brand blueprint you created with the Brand Thinking Canvas.

GOALS — Name the most important goals for your organisation in the coming period and how you think branding can help achieve them.

CHALLENGE — What creative work do you need in order to achieve this?

ASSIGNMENT — What are you asking the creative team to deliver in order to assist you in reaching this goal? Be exact! (Strategic review? Name? Logo? Copywriting? Info graphics? Ad campaign?)

OUTPUT — What are you expecting as the tangible outcome of this project? (For example: strategic recommendation on doubling your brand audience, a logoset, the visual design of a website, or a communication plan for 2016.)

ABOUT THE CREATIVE PROCESS

DECISION MAKER — Who is the person who gives the final yes/no on work? How will they judge success?

PROCESS — How would you like to be involved?
What type of relationship would you like to build?

LEGAL — Who will become the owner of the created work? Is it confidential? Who will arrange possible legal checks on trademarking the work?

PLANNING — What is the timing of the project?
When is the final delivery needed?
What are the intermediate deadlines along the way?

BUDGET — Do you have an indication of budget or a specific request on how you would like financial proposals to be structured?

STEP 2
MAKE SURE IT IS YOURS TO KEEP

Before going all the way, make sure your name can be legally protected through a trademark, and that it is available as a straightforward domain name and consistent social media handles across platforms.

TRADEMARKING TAKES TIME

Researching your brand name's availability can take a number of weeks or even months, especially if you want to register it in different countries. Make sure you calculate this into your planning. It can be beneficial to check a shortlist of favourites so you do not lose time when you cannot claim the name you love best. To be absolutely safe, also claim all the social media and domain names on your shortlist. Be kind to others and set them free again if you don't use them.

TRADEMARKING
Read more about protecting your brand in the guest essay by Marleen Splinter on page 206.

STEP 3
CREATE A BRAND BOOK

In this stage you want all the brand development work to be captured in a brand book. A brand book allows everyone who works with your brand to build the brand expressions that make you stand out from the crowd. It contains your strategic work (insights, positioning, brand blueprint) and your creative work (messaging, visual identity elements, communication examples). You can even go so far as to include a manual with in-depth instructions on how to create messages and design items.

ALL SHAPES AND SIZES

Brand books can come in all shapes and sizes, from physical, paper books, to PDF's to online portals. They can be instructional or inspirational. Some come in eight pages or a poster, others are hundreds of pages long. Some focus on values and company culture, others on design finesse. Want to take a peek at some examples? Many brand manuals of brands are readily accessible online. A quick online search for 'brand book', 'brand manual' or 'brand toolkit' will give you lots of examples. We love the IDEO 'Little book of Values' for its simple, articulate language and beautiful visuals that show how values drive behaviour at IDEO. The EasyGroup brand manual is a good example of a straightforward functional guideline.

If you are a one-person organisation working with one designer, a brand book might not be needed. But as soon as your team grows and you start working with several designers, copywriters and producers, a brand book is a really great asset to have.

WHY A BRAND BOOK?
A brand book helps to:

» Align your team internally and give them the power to execute the brand and bring it to life.
» Ensure technical consistency (for instance, colours look the same on each printed brochure, screen and physical object).
» Ensure creative consistency so the look and feel of your brand is the same across different items made by different parties.

WHAT IS IN A BRAND BOOK?
A brand book can contain of the following elements:

Brand strategy
• Inspirational: your brand blueprint told as a story
• Functional: your brand blueprint in different steps: insight, market, positioning, brand core (essence, vision, mission, values, brand promises).

Verbal identity
• Name and payoff use
• Tone of voice guidelines
• Messaging or communication guidelines
• Audio guidelines (music, sound logo, voiceover)

Visual identity
• Logo, colour, typography
• Iconography, graphic elements
• Photography or illustration style
• Layout look and feel
• Motion guidelines
• Benchmark examples
• Guidelines on use of the above

The brand book contains instructions and refers to source files placed on a website or server where people can access them for use (optionally password protected).

• Logoset: pixel (.jpg, .png) and vector file format (.ai, .eps), regular and diapositive, in colour and black and white, full logo and stacked logo or icon, social media avatars. Files come in the following colour settings: RGB (screen), CMYK (full-colour printing), Pantone (special printing)
• Colour palette swatches: RGB, CMYK, Pantone
• Photography or illustration database of ready-to-use materials
• Iconography in vector/pixel and in different colour formats
• Design templates: Basic templates for correspondence (for instance, Microsoft Office: letterhead, PowerPoint), templates for printed work (brochures, flyers) and digital work (newsletters, social media formats).

STEP 4
DESIGN FIRST EXPERIENCES

They say you only have one chance to make a first impression. Make it count! Develop the first fundamental interactions that are crucial to impressing your core audience. A professional website that you can now refer people to. Business cards, a brochure or other tangible items you can leave behind with people. A first blogpost series or 3-minute explanatory video. A well-designed pitch deck for your presentation to investors. Keep it lean – there will be plenty of time to do more in the brand building phase!

WHERE DOES THAT MISSION/VISION STUFF GO?

What to do with the brand core elements? Do you plop them on a web page? There is no one rule as to where brand core elements 'go'. Some organisations use them purely as internal documentation. Their creatives translate the vision, mission and values into actions and communications without explicitly mentioning them. Others literally paint their vision on the office wall so all team members know what the purpose of their work is.

WALK THE WALK

Despite being passionate about social or environmental change, many organisations don't consider the sustainable or ethical consequences of their branded materials such as flyers, shirts, caps, pens or notebooks (called brand swag). Why should your swag be excluded from your ambitions for positive impact? Giving away $10 T-shirts made in Bangladesh and $1 plastic pens is probably at odds with your mission. Consider giving away more durable brand swag. For instance, a refillable water bottle or eco-friendly notebooks. People will use them for a long time, take them wherever they go and show off your brand while doing so.

BRAND PITCH TEMPLATE

You will have countless opportunities to pitch what you do: at events or conferences, on a chance elevator ride or during a lunch or business meeting. When you have one simple, strong pitch ready for these moments you leave a strong impression while not having to craft something new at each opportunity.

WHAT IT'S FOR

» Translating your brand strategy to a quick pitch that you have memorised for presentations and chance encounters with potential partners, clients, investors and press.

» Making a big impression.

HOW TO USE IT

» Use the template and the work you have done in the brand thinking stage to structure your story.

» Memorise it so you can easily and naturally reproduce it under all circumstances (even when someone wakes you up during the night!). When you work with a team, it can be a great advantage if everyone knows the pitch as well.

» You can turn it into a short video or document you can share.

EXAMPLE: INTERNET OF ELEPHANTS

WHAT IS THE PROBLEM YOU ARE ADDRESSING?

We are facing the rapid extinction of wildlife and we only have two sources to fund the conservation battle: ecotourism and fundraising. Ecotourism is only for a small group of people who can afford it. Fundraising only reaches the already converted. There is a far wider audience of people who love animals but who are not actively involved in conservation. We need to reach them in order to reverse the tide.

WHAT IS YOUR INSIGHT?

People lead busy lives with lots of things competing for their attention. We need to meet them where they already are. The loss of an entire species is too abstract for people. They do respond when individual animals like Cecil the lion die.

WHO YOU ARE

We are Internet of Elephants, a Kenya/US-based startup.

WHAT YOU DO

We develop online games that use the data of individual wild animals to reach a massive global audience.

WHY IT MATTERS

Emotional connections between people and wildlife are crucial to winning the conservation battle. We want to see 20 million people wake up in the morning to see how their elephant is doing. A popular platform such as games helps us reach a massive new audience and generate a new source of revenue for conservation.

....

YOUR ASK

This is the dynamic part of the pitch. You adapt the ask to each audience you pitch to at different stages of your journey.

We are looking for test gamers to play our first game prototype.

We are looking for investors who want to support business model innovation in conservation.

We are looking for a Chief Traction Officer that can help us get 20 million active players.

STEP 5
LAUNCH!

Choose a day for your brand to go public. It can be a big bang or the start of a gradual roll-out, but on this one day, your brand will see the light. Make sure your first designed items are ready to be revealed. You can use the opportunity to bring people together (online/offline) and get people talking about your brand, potentially even generate some first PR. Keep in mind: just launching a brand does not generate excitement. When a launch has purpose beyond generating publicity, it will be more appealing to your audiences as well as the press.

GETTING PUBLICITY
Read more about building a relationship with reporters in the guest essay by Simon Buckby on page 202.

EVENTS
Designing an event with purpose is a great way to get on people's radar. Read more about how events can help you build momentum on page 90.

PHASE 4
BRAND BUILDING

A brand is never finished: brand building is the ongoing process of activating your brand through meaningful interaction.

1. COMMUNICATE
Stay in the conversation and lead it! Every year you will have numerous occasions to talk about what you are doing, share ideas and build your leadership.

2. ACTIVATE
Here is your chance to create a rich spectrum of experiences for your audiences.

3. BUILD BRAND AMBASSADORS
Inside and outside your organisation.

4. MANAGE BRAND ARCHITECTURE
When your brand is a success, sooner or later you will launch a new product or service and the question will arise: do we need to launch it as a new brand? Think before you create a second brand.

5. EVOLVE
A brand is a living organism that needs constant upkeep. If something doesn't work, iterate! If something can be improved, evolve it!

STEP 1
COMMUNICATE

This is where the rubber hits the road: in order for your brand to reach the audiences it deserves, you need to get your message out there. This is where a marketing/communication strategy comes in. This strategy will guide your advertising, content development, social media communications, speaking engagements and more.

They say, 'If you build it, they will come', but this is rarely the case when it comes to new brands. You can set up shop, but until you have actual interactions with people, your brand will exist in a vacuum. Expecting people to magically discover you on their own is a grave mistake. You will need to build a marketing/communications strategy.

Creating such a strategy is a complex activity that requires a toolkit of its own. Find a basic overview of your options below. If your budget allows it, find a marketing or communications specialist to develop your strategy and one person to execute it over time.

COMMUNICATIONS
Throughout the year, you will find or create opportunities for communication. Perhaps you will report on new developments, share your knowledge, share events or product updates or new launches. Ensuring your team has a reporter's mindset makes it easy to generate regular and fresh communications. Keeping your supporters up to date regularly and remaining in view helps to build the brand recognition you need. The most common communication channels are newsletters, social media and your website/blog. Don't forget to include a communication strategy towards investors, donors and partners. They might not be your core audience but they are crucial to keep up to date! Creating a communications calendar helps to keep the overview.

MOST STARTUPS DON'T FAIL BECAUSE THEY CAN'T BUILD A PRODUCT. MOST STARTUPS FAIL BECAUSE THEY CAN'T GET TRACTION.
—GABRIEL WEINBERG & JUSTIN MARES

 DIGITAL MARKETING
All the options available in digital marketing can be overwhelming. Read the guest essay by Ben Matthews on page 212.

MARKETING

Marketing is the activity of promoting and selling your offer. You can do this through a wide variety of channels. There is direct marketing (email, post), social media marketing, content marketing (creating demand for your product by producing content such as stories, videos, blogs), digital marketing, promotional teams on the street, and dozens of other avenues. Digital marketing used for the onboarding of users into a digital service is often referred to as 'growth hacking' or 'creating traction'. Methods vary in effectivity per industry and depend on where your audiences can be found.

ADVERTISING

Traditional brand building mechanisms like paid advertising are no longer the obvious option. When interviewing our case study subjects, we noticed none of them had chosen mass media advertising or any paid advertising at all until they were well into their third year or beyond. Some have never paid for any advertising whatsoever. And it makes sense. The brand building field is democratising, and social media and content strategy are replacing the bought media at a rapid pace. Nevertheless, although spreading the word purely through your own channels and network is free, it is hard work. Each avenue of communication requires you to master a different skill set if you want to really make it work for you. This makes it very labour intensive. Therefore, social media ads that quickly attract many likes and follows (for what that is worth) are gaining momentum fast.

Just because advertising is no longer the first option for many businesses does not mean that it never has its place. For organisations that have larger budgets and an operational model that allows them to offer products or services effectively at high volume, there can be a lot of benefits to advertising. Like marketing, advertising has a wide range of channels. Think about: radio advertising & podcast sponsorship, street and public transport advertising, social media ads and sponsoring (sports teams/events).

TRACTION CHANNELS

For most organisations, marketing and communication serve to grow their customer or user base. The process of onboarding customers is called 'creating traction'. In their book: *TRACTION: How Any Startup Can Achieve Explosive Customer Growth*, authors Gabriel Weinberg and Justin Mares identify 19 channels to create traction.

Targeting Blogs • Publicity • Unconventional PR
Search Engine Marketing • Social and Display Ads
Offline Ads • Search Engine Optimisation
Content Marketing • Email Marketing
Viral Marketing • Engineering as Marketing
Business Development • Sales • Affiliate Programmes
Existing Platforms • Trade Shows • Offline Events
Speaking Engagements • Community Building

Weinberg and Mares promote the idea that each startup should test these 19 channels methodically to see which move the dial and consequently invest your resources in that channel. The book gives you a step-by-step method in doing so and comes highly recommended!

HOW OTHERS MANAGE ADVERTISING
The case studies of Sugru (page 53) and Soko (page 56) describe their journey into advertising.

STEP 2
ACTIVATE!

Make sure you don't think only in communications, but in actions too. Building a brand is not just talking the talk but also walking the walk! Here is your chance to bring the brand to life in everything you do. How does your brand translate to your HR policy? Which people will you put in the spotlight? Can you design an event? Go back to the ideas you developed in the Brand Thinking Canvas to see which ones you can realise. Investigate which actions and communications have the highest impact/feasibility ratio and make a plan to execute those.

TOOL
ACTION RANKING

After brainstorming on brand building concepts you have a list of ideas. Which should you execute? The action ranking model helps you prioritise.

WHAT IT'S FOR

» Prioritising actions and communications based on the best combination of feasibility and impact.

HOW TO USE IT

» Draw the axes on a whiteboard or paper.
» Place your ideas on a sticky note in one of the fields.
» To assess feasibility, ask yourself if you have the budget, time and people power to execute? How likely is it to happen if it depends on others?
» To assess impact, make a common sense estimate of the chance of connecting with the people you want to reach and of how much that will help you in reaching your goals.
» The top right corner offers you the best chances. The top left can be 'low hanging fruit' to execute swiftly and easily. The right bottom field is for daredevils.

FEASIBILITY

start tweeting on our topic

get personal intro to Fast Company journalist

HIGH FEASIBILITY LOW IMPACT

HIGH FEASIBILITY HIGH IMPACT

place ad in local paper

create unique community event

partnership with Kiva

create a global AdWords campaign

IMPACT

start pen pal programme

LOW FEASIBILITY LOW IMPACT

LOW FEASIBILITY HIGH IMPACT

take entire company on field trip to see work in action

win Nobel Prize

STEP 3
BUILD BRAND AMBASSADORS

You want every person on your team to be a brand ambassador. Every interaction they have with your audience contributes to how people think and feel about your brand. From your board of directors and your partners to the person picking up the phone, interns and volunteers, everyone in your organisation matters in building positive brand associations. Your ambassadors are not just team members! Empower enthusiastic external fans and supporters to become brand ambassadors themselves. These days, a brand is as strong as the communities it can galvanise.

HUMANS WANTED

Kenyan/US-based tech for wildlife startup Internet of Elephants has deliberately chosen to co-create their games with the public. They build prototypes and make them available to get feedback on the game while simultaneously building a base of followers and fans.

SUGRU

Read the case study on Sugru to learn more about how they built a tribe of supporters on page 53.

CROWDFUNDING AS A BRANDING TOOL

Crowdfunding has become a great way of building a community and support around your product, service or cause. It helps you to galvanise support from your existing audience and to spread it to new ones.

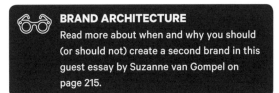

STEP 4
MANAGE BRAND ARCHITECTURE

When your brand is a success, sooner or later you will launch a new product or service and the question will arise: do we need to launch it as a new brand? The structure of brands within an organisation is called brand architecture. Think twice before you create a second brand and start to build a complex brand architecture. Managing multiple brands is resource draining and should be considered from all angles before any decisions are made.

BRAND ARCHITECTURE
Read more about when and why you should (or should not) create a second brand in this guest essay by Suzanne van Gompel on page 215.

BRAND ARCHITECTURE DECISION TREE

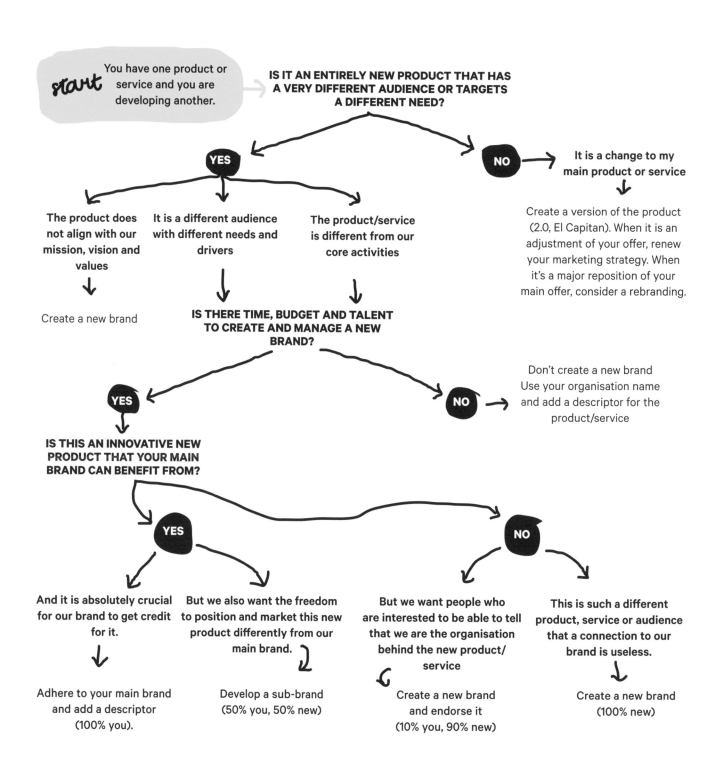

start You have one product or service and you are developing another.

IS IT AN ENTIRELY NEW PRODUCT THAT HAS A VERY DIFFERENT AUDIENCE OR TARGETS A DIFFERENT NEED?

YES

NO → It is a change to my main product or service

Create a version of the product (2.0, El Capitan). When it is an adjustment of your offer, renew your marketing strategy. When it's a major reposition of your main offer, consider a rebranding.

The product does not align with our mission, vision and values

Create a new brand

It is a different audience with different needs and drivers

The product/service is different from our core activities

IS THERE TIME, BUDGET AND TALENT TO CREATE AND MANAGE A NEW BRAND?

YES

NO → Don't create a new brand Use your organisation name and add a descriptor for the product/service

IS THIS AN INNOVATIVE NEW PRODUCT THAT YOUR MAIN BRAND CAN BENEFIT FROM?

YES

NO

And it is absolutely crucial for our brand to get credit for it.

Adhere to your main brand and add a descriptor (100% you).

But we also want the freedom to position and market this new product differently from our main brand.

Develop a sub-brand (50% you, 50% new)

But we want people who are interested to be able to tell that we are the organisation behind the new product/service

Create a new brand and endorse it (10% you, 90% new)

This is such a different product, service or audience that a connection to our brand is useless.

Create a new brand (100% new)

STEP 5
EVOLVE

Change is the only certainty you have: you will evolve as an organisation, you will understand your audience better and you will evolve your brand and communications accordingly. If something doesn't work, iterate! If something can be improved, evolve it! Your brand's core will most likely stay the same, but the way in which you express it should be able to grow based on the lessons you learn as you go. More fundamentally, your product or service's context will change, new competitors will emerge and your audiences' lives will change. A strong brand keeps its ear to the ground so that it can grow and adapt to these changes. When your insight or proposition is no longer relevant, your existence is at risk.

THE WAR ROOM

It can be hard to keep track of all your brand interactions throughout the year and even harder to be strict about evaluation and learning. Digital is fleeting and events follow each other at a rapid pace. You want to keep an eye on whether things are aligned, what was successful and what your learnings are. To make things easier to grasp, create a dedicated war room where you gather photos and prints of all your activities and communications. Gather photo materials, ads, brochures, blog posts, social media headers, press, public speaking outlines etc. If you want to compare yourself to the competition or to a benchmark, reserve one wall for them.

CHECKUP
Use the brand checkup exercise on page 198 to see if your brand is still up to date.

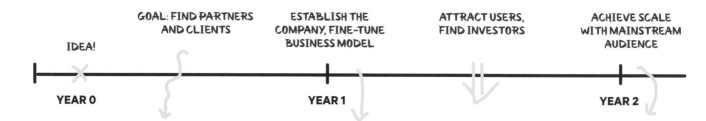

YEAR 0		YEAR 1		YEAR 2
IDEA!	GOAL: FIND PARTNERS AND CLIENTS	ESTABLISH THE COMPANY, FINE-TUNE BUSINESS MODEL	ATTRACT USERS, FIND INVESTORS	ACHIEVE SCALE WITH MAINSTREAM AUDIENCE

Pitch! Pitch! Pitch! Get my storytelling right. Create a brand blueprint, create a lean brand identity and first communications to look credible and get people interested. Organise a small-scale event to test concepts and get PR. Write blogs/essays on my mission on media platforms where potential partners hang out.

We only have a pilot project to sell, but we are going live! Solid website and channels. Starting to build a following online. Testing different brand promises with our audiences.

Adapt our brand: we now know what we truly want to be recognised for! Create clear & compelling brand promises. Enlist network to increase sign-ups for the product and convince investors.

 Create killer digital presentation and video to support pitching.

Invest in big marketing push. Set up Brand Team internally. Create unique photography style to increase our recognisability on social media.

Branding doesn't exist purely for its own sake. The time and resources you commit to branding should provide you with a return on investment in reaching your objectives.

You will invest a lot of time and resources into your branding and that alone is a reason to make sure that you are using it to reach your goals, whether short term and practical (recruiting the best talent for your team, creating more loyalty among your suppliers) or long term and visionary (increasing your social impact, boosting your finances).

THE BRAND THINKING CANVAS
Use your brand thinking skills to develop new ideas for products and services and other brand interactions and let your brand lead innovation! See pages 168-171.

BRAND DEVELOPMENT SHOULD SUPPORT BUSINESS DEVELOPMENT

As your organisation grows and changes, your goals change with it. You might provide different services, or reach different audiences. You might need different things from different people. Your brand has to evolve with you, so take time every 6–12 months to look at your brand strategy and see what you can improve so you keep moving forward.

CHAPTER 5
TOOL TEMPLATES

HOW TO USE THE TOOL TEMPLATES

Each tool on the following pages comes with instructions on the left side of the page.

While using the tools, keep these best practices in mind:

» Don't write directly on the materials but use sticky notes so you can adapt answers easily and change them as you go along.

» If all goes well, your brand will evolve over time and stickies will make it easier to reuse the materials.

» Use a black marker on the sticky notes for your ideas. This forces you to keep things compact.

» If possible work with the tools collaboratively. If you work solo, check outcomes with trusted colleagues, friends, partners or mentors, to do a reality check and to get extra input and insights.

» Document the results with a camera or scan them to files.

» Keep your work in your sight so you can use it as a reference for your daily work.

What else you need:

» Sticky notes or Stattys notes

» Black markers

» Plenty of wall space

» Tape or magnets to put things up on the wall

» A camera (or phone) to capture results

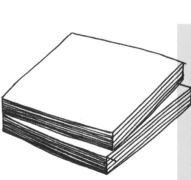

👍 TOOLS ARE FOR BRAINSTORMING

There are not a lot of wrong answers, but there are plenty of unoriginal or uninspiring ones. Make sure you don't just fill in the blanks. For example, when you are asked to think of communication channels, don't just write down 'Twitter', but how you will use it to reach your audiences: what do you share, what is your tone of voice, how do you interact, who do you support online?

TOOL
INSIGHT
GENERATOR

You have an insight into how change can be created. You've made an observation, you see a dilemma people are struggling with. There is an unmet need that you can provide in. This insight will drive your brand.

WHAT IT'S FOR

» Defining the insight that drives what you do.

HOW TO USE IT

» Express your insight as observation, dilemma, need.
» Start at your observation and work downwards.
» Capture your insight in one phrase that will become the foundation for your next steps.
» Test is with your audiences. Does it resonate with them? Do they recognise the dilemma and the need? Does the way it is articulated appeal to them? Test your insight through a structured testing process with respondents or pitch it one on one.
» If needed, adapt and test again.

OBSERVATION

An observation or fact about a problem in the world which is recognisable for your audience.

DILEMMA

Something that stops people from doing or feeling the right thing.

NEED

Articulation of what can be done to improve the situation.

IN SHORT

Frame your insight in one compelling phrase.

TOOL
PERSONA TEMPLATE

A persona is a fictional profile that represents a brand audience. Developing a persona helps you to bring the audience to life.

WHAT IT'S FOR

» Clarifying your ideas about and relationships with your audiences.

» Personalising your audiences and giving them a presence in your thinking and planning.

HOW TO USE IT

» Do research into the world of your primary audience. Interview them, go to where they hang out.

» Create a fictional persona for one or more people representative of the group.

» Keep it simple. Work with a maximum of three to five personas.

» Make them real and compelling. Avoid clichés. Use a photo (of someone you don't know) that fits the profile and brings the fictional persona to life.

NAME + AGE

LIVES IN

PRIVATE LIFE

PROFESSIONAL EXPERIENCE

Job title

Organisation

Other experiences (past jobs, volunteer work)

Educational background

ACTIVITY & BEHAVIOUR

Generation which…

His/her role model is…

A well-known emotion

Geographical orientation

NEEDS

Pains

Gains

Information wants / needs

QUOTE

Something you would hear him/her say

SOCIAL & TECH

Tech literacy level

Hardware

Social media

INTERACTIONS

Places

Events

Communication channels

BRAND THINKING CANVAS #1

The Brand Thinking Canvas represents the holistic anatomy of a brand. It helps you define your brand and brainstorm the myriad ways you can bring it to life.

WHAT IT'S FOR

» Defining the core of your brand, what it is that drives your actions and communications.
» Creating awareness on how this can be translated to the outside through a visual and verbal identity.
» Brainstorming great interactions.

HOW TO USE IT

» Use the empty template on the right (scaled for use on A4).
» Work from the inside out: start from the core (vision, mission, values, promises and essence) to the identity and interactions.
» Use sticky notes for your answers.
» Keep it short. If you start to see entire paragraphs or bullet lists appear on a sticky note, you are working in too much detail.
» Keep the canvas on a wall for you and your team to keep the big picture in sight (literally).

DIGITAL VERSION

The Brand Thinking Canvas is available on poster size at www.the-brandling.com/brandthinkingcanvas
Download the digital version for free by using the discount code 'bisreaders2' at checkout.

PRODUCTS & SERVICES
What do you offer?

TECHNOLOGY
What hardware or software can support interaction with your audiences?

PLACES & EVENTS
Where are you located? Where do you need to be seen?
What events can you develop, attend or be a part of?

VISUAL IDENTITY
How does your brand translate to your appearance? Example: logo, colour palette, typography, photography, illustration style, materials, overall look and feel.

BRAND PROMISES
What do you commit to deliver to your primary audience?

VISION What is the world that you wish to see?

BRAND ESSENCE
The reason you exist, distilled into a compact, compelling phrase.

VALUES What are the principles that guide your decisions?

MISSION What do you do to work towards your vision?

PEOPLE, TALENT & BEHAVIOUR
Who is the face of your organisation?
Which type of talent do you want to hire?

How does your brand translate to your verbal expression? Example: naming, payoff/slogan, tone of voice, messaging.

COMMUNICATION & CHANNELS
How will you communicate and through which channels?
How will you use them, what is your topic and what do you say?

VERBAL IDENTITY

Who are your natural allies? With whom do you share values, audiences or services?
How can you use them to build your brand?

PARTNERSHIPS & COLLABORATIONS

BRAND THINKING CANVAS #2

Part 2 of the Brand Thinking Canvas helps you create ideas to get your brand on the radar of your different audiences.

WHAT IT'S FOR
» Mapping out who your audiences are.
» Defining what you want them to think and feel about you.
» Brainstorming how you can achieve that.

HOW TO USE IT
» Copy your brand essence from the Brand Thinking Canvas part one.
» Map out the different audiences you need to make your product, services or idea a success.
» Start with your primary audience at the top and continue clockwise with the secondary audiences.
» First identify all the audiences, then dive into the what and the how per audience.
» First, define what you want them to recognise you for.
» Second, how you will achieve that recognition: through which actions and communications?

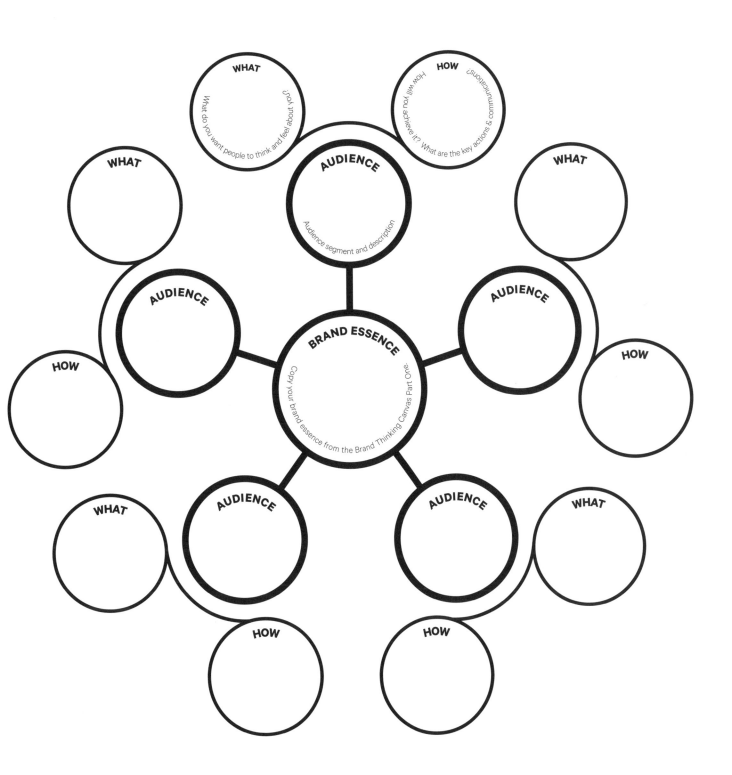

WHAT

What do you want people to think and feel about you?

HOW

How will you achieve it? What are the key actions & communications?

WHAT

AUDIENCE

Audience segment and description

WHAT

AUDIENCE

BRAND ESSENCE

Copy your brand essence from the Brand Thinking Canvas Part One.

AUDIENCE

HOW

HOW

WHAT

AUDIENCE

AUDIENCE

WHAT

HOW

HOW

TOOL
THE CLIMB

YOUR VISION

THE WORLD YOU WANT TO SEE

'I want to see a forest full of trees.'

Often people get their mission and vision confused. The Climb Tool helps you get it right.

WHAT IT'S FOR

» Defining your mission and vision.

HOW TO USE IT

» Start with your vision, the destination of your climb. What is the change that you want to see in the world?
» Work backwards from your vision towards your mission by defining how you will get to the top of the hill.
By which means? Offering what type of value?

What does the world look like that you want to help create? What will the lives of your audience look like when you successfully deliver your product or service?

YOUR MISSION

WHAT YOU DO TO MAKE IT HAPPEN

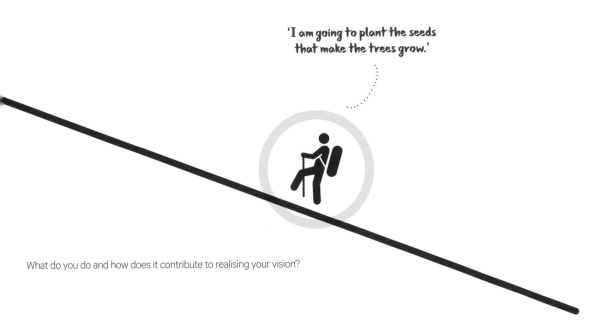

'I am going to plant the seeds that make the trees grow.'

What do you do and how does it contribute to realising your vision?

TOOL
MISSION COMPOSER

A mission statement is an effective way of getting your audiences to truly understand what you do, why you do it, and why it is important.

WHAT IT'S FOR

» Clarifying what you do, for whom and why.
» Galvanising support.

HOW TO USE IT

» Follow the arrows.
» Can't find the right words? Use thesaurus.com to find alternatives.
» Wordsmith sentences by writing each word on one sticky note to form a sentence and place alternatives beneath it.
» Summarise your mission in one short, compelling sentence.
» Use the extended mission statement (in the dotted yellow circles) as a structure for pitches to investors, partners, clients or funders. Add an ask or a call to action for them at the end.

WHAT IS THE PROBLEM YOU ARE ADDRESSING?

SUMMARISE!

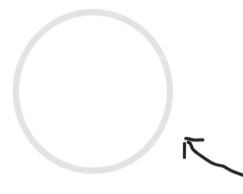

What is your mission in one short, compelling sentence?

WHO YOU ARE

This is where you come in!

WHAT YOU DO

WHY IT MATTERS

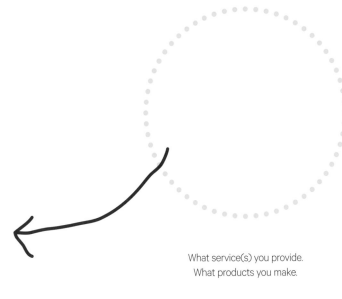

What service(s) you provide.
What products you make.

How you resolve the problem
in the first circle.

TOOL
GOAL SETTING

Change never happens without several people getting involved. By listing your goals you will uncover your brands audiences.

WHAT IT'S FOR

» Uncovering your brands different audiences.

HOW TO USE IT

» Start with where you are now (Point A).
» List what defines your current situation. Use these guiding questions to jumpstart your thinking: What is the 'status' of the status quo you want to change? Who do you need to know about what you are trying to achieve? Who is on your team? Who is funding your business: customers, clients, investors? Are you well known? Is anyone spreading the word about what you do?
» Think about a mid-term horizon of about three years as your future scenario (Point B).
» List what the answers on the left should look like in the future. Don't just think about what is feasible, think about what is desirable.
» Make your answers specific and concrete.
» Identify the audiences that are needed to achieve your goals.

B **WHERE YOU WANT TO GO**

C **AUDIENCES**

TOOL
ACTION PLANNER

Once you know what you need to do, don't let any of your insights slip away! Create an action plan that gives you an easy overview.

WHAT IT'S FOR

» Capturing what needs to be done in order to achieve your goals.

» Helping you get organised and ensuring that you put your thoughts into action.

HOW TO USE IT

» Fill it out after each major brand strategy session where you've come up with ideas on how to build your brand.

» Make it extremely specific and tangible.

» Update it continuously.

ACTIONS What you will do to get there	RESOURCES Who & what you need to get it done	DEADLINE When should it be accomplished

TOOL
ACTION RANKING

After brainstorming on brand building concepts you have a list of ideas. Which should you execute? The action ranking model helps you prioritise.

WHAT IT'S FOR
» Prioritising actions and communications based on the best combination of feasibility and impact.

HOW TO USE IT
» Place your ideas on a sticky note in one of the fields.
» To assess feasibility, ask yourself if you have the budget, time and people power to execute? How likely is it to happen if it depends on others?
» To assess impact, make a common sense estimate of the chance of connecting with the people you want to reach and of how much that will help you in reaching your goals.
» The top right corner offers you the best chances. The top left can be 'low hanging fruit' to execute swiftly and easily. The right bottom field is for daredevils.

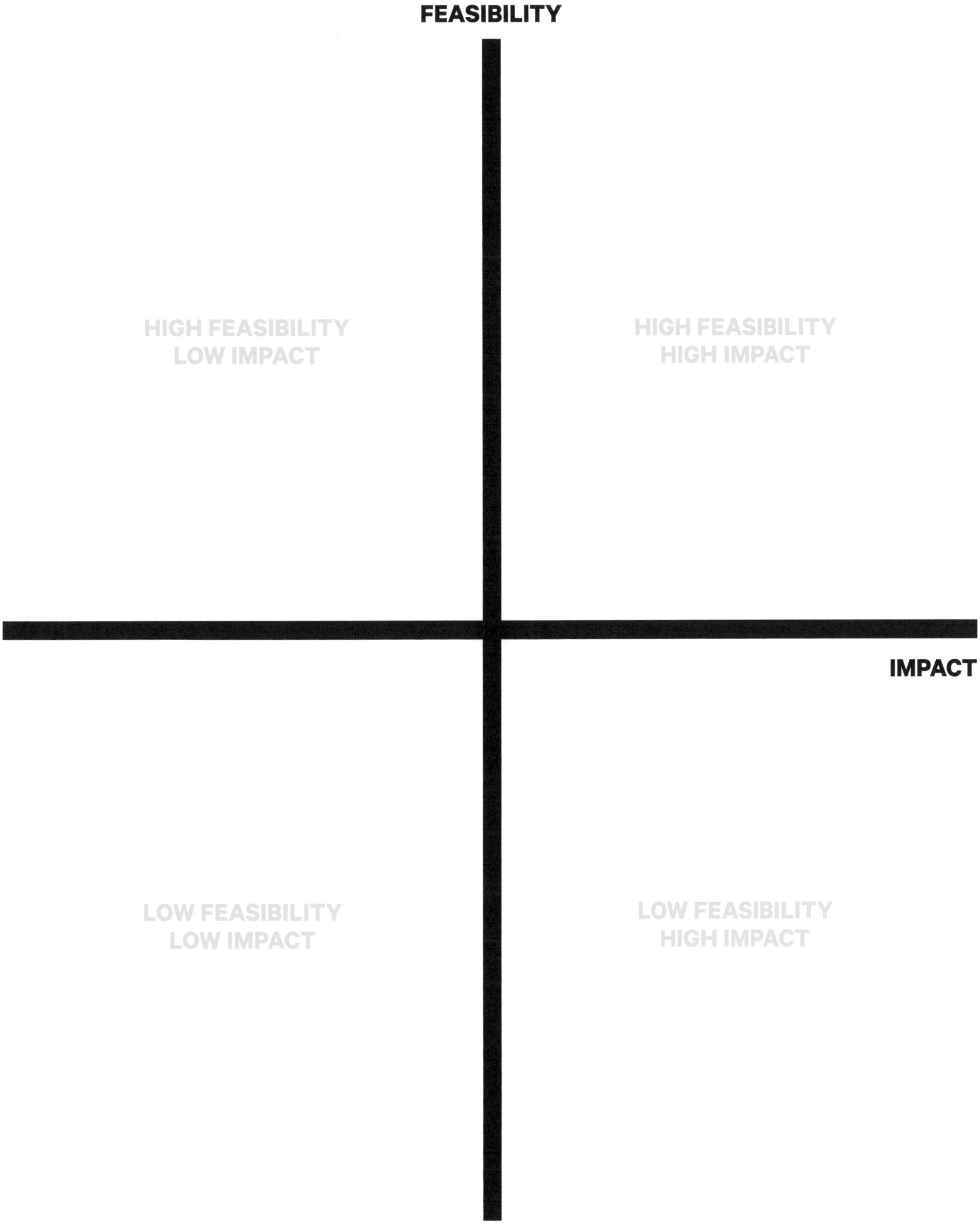

FEASIBILITY

HIGH FEASIBILITY
LOW IMPACT

HIGH FEASIBILITY
HIGH IMPACT

IMPACT

LOW FEASIBILITY
LOW IMPACT

LOW FEASIBILITY
HIGH IMPACT

TOOL
BRAND PITCH
TEMPLATE

You will have countless opportunities to pitch what you do: at events or conferences, on a chance elevator ride or during a lunch or business meeting. When you have one simple, strong pitch ready for these moments you leave a strong impression while not having to craft something new at each opportunity.

WHAT IT'S FOR
» Translating your brand strategy to a quick pitch that you have memorised for presentations and chance encounters with potential partners, clients, investors and press.
» Making a big impression.

HOW TO USE IT
» Use the template and the work you have done in the brand thinking stage to structure your story.
» Memorise it so you can easily and naturally reproduce it under all circumstances (even when someone wakes you up during the night!). When you work with a team, it can be a great advantage if everyone knows the pitch as well.
» You can turn it into a short video or document you can share.

**WHAT IS THE PROBLEM
YOU ARE ADDRESSING?**

WHAT IS YOUR INSIGHT?

WHO YOU ARE

WHAT YOU DO

WHY IT MATTERS

....

YOUR ASK

This is the dynamic part of the pitch.
You adapt the ask to each audience you
pitch to at different stages of your journey.

TOOL
THE LADDER

When you are defining a brand promise for customers, the ladder helps you to move up from a functional promise (what) to an impactful promise (why) at three different levels.

WHAT IT'S FOR

» Easing into progressing from a functional promise to a more emotional value for your audiences.
» Brainstorm brand promises.

HOW TO USE IT

» Start at the bottom step and work your way up.

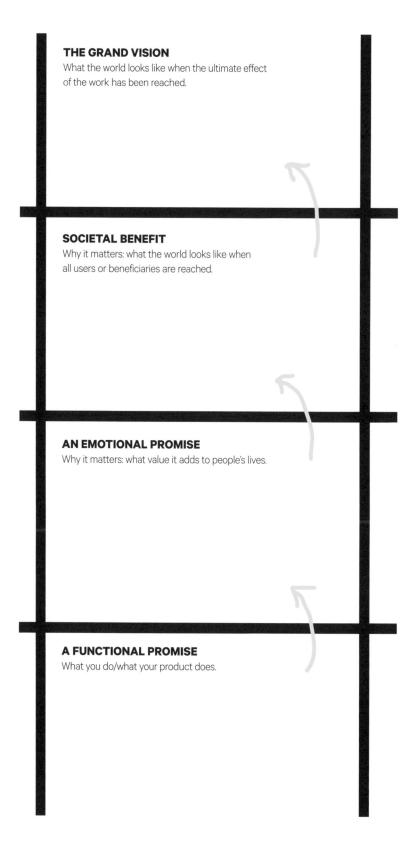

THE GRAND VISION
What the world looks like when the ultimate effect of the work has been reached.

SOCIETAL BENEFIT
Why it matters: what the world looks like when all users or beneficiaries are reached.

AN EMOTIONAL PROMISE
Why it matters: what value it adds to people's lives.

A FUNCTIONAL PROMISE
What you do/what your product does.

CHAPTER 6
EXERCISES

EXERCISE
SPOT THE
INSIGHT

Insights are all around us. Hone your skills at defining a compelling insight by spotting them in ads, commercials, brochures and even political speeches.

WHAT IT'S FOR

» Build your understanding of what an insight is and how they are translated to communications.

HOW TO USE IT

» Make a habit of scanning advertisements online, in the paper, magazines or on TV.
» Analyse three or more of the examples on the right.
» What is the product or service being sold?
» What is the belief about the world that is being communicated?
» What is the dilemma that the audience faces?
» What is the need that the product/ service addresses?
» How is the insight translated to the brand and its communications?
» What can you learn from these examples?

Go to the website of Tesla electric cars

Watch a Chipotle animation

Go to Generosity.com and read their mission statement

Watch the TED Talk by Jane McGonigal: The game that can give you 10 extra years of life

Check out the Omo laundry detergent commercial 'Dirt is Good' on YouTube

Watch the TED Talk of Dr Ayana Johnson or visit her website

EXERCISE
MAP OUT YOUR MARKET

Everyone operates in a market. It can be a crowded market, a niche or an entirely open market. Either way, the goal is to position yourself in a unique spot in the market.

WHAT IT'S FOR
» Understanding your market and how you can uniquely position your brand.
» Informing the brand development work so you can stand out from the crowd.

HOW TO USE IT
» Consider the defining characteristics of your market based on your brand proposition to your audience.
» Experiment with several polar opposites that tie them together. This creates a field that represents your market.
» Place the names of the competition on a location along the axis.
» Your insight should allow you to place yourself on the map in a unique spot.
» If you are not uniquely positioned, get more specific or experiment with other characteristics.
» Adding the competition's logos will help you to get a good perspective on how you can stand out visually.

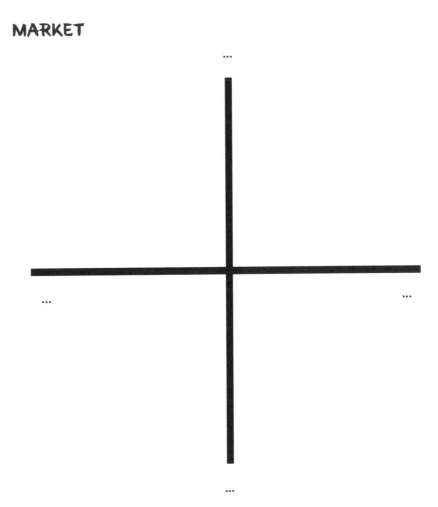

MARKET

EXERCISE
ANALYSE THE COMPETITION

If you want to develop a brand that stands out from the crowd, you need to know what the competition offers, looks like, how it speaks and which interactions it capitalises on.

WHAT IT'S FOR

» Understanding who you need to differentiate yourself from and how.
» Informing your work on the brand core, identity and interactions.
» Briefing your team and copywriter, brand agency or designer in the brand making phase.

HOW TO USE IT

» Take the closest competitors from your market map exercise. Use the checklist on the right to gather the brand assets.
» Create a collage/case study for each competitor.
» Gather the materials in a presentation file.
» Which brand do you think is particularly successful that you can learn from?
» Identify any common threads between the different competitors that you can differentiate from.
» You can use the materials in a later stage when you brief your branding agency.

CHECKLIST

Proposition
Reasons to believe
(impact, result, proof, testimonials)
Pricing (high/low)
Reputation

VISUAL IDENTITY
Logo
Font
Colours
Photography
(what do they show, what is the style)
Illustrations,
(motion) graphics

VERBAL IDENTITY
Name
Payoff
Tone of voice, editorial formula
(what do they talk about, how do they talk about it)
Key messages

INTERACTIONS
Products & services
Places & events
Communication & channels
Partnerships & collaborations
People, talent & behaviour
Technology

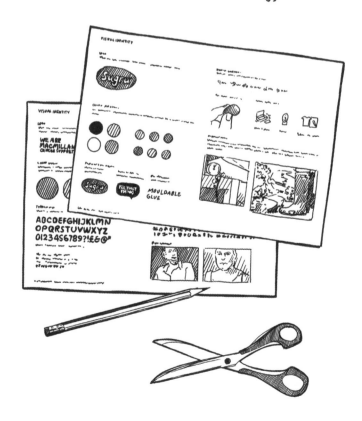

EXERCISE
VISUALISE YOUR VISION

Imagining the world you want to see is not easy! To capture a future and make it tangible requires a lot of imagination and guts. Visualising it makes it easier!

WHAT IT'S FOR
» Make your vision tangible and actionable.

HOW TO USE IT
» First you need to set the stage where you want to see change. Imagine the world, society, the lives of your audience, your industry, a city or place.
» Sketch out what you would like it to look like. Get very practical about it.
» Imagine the future as a city of your dreams, a group of people, or a day in the life of an individual.
» What do they do, what do they use, what do they feel like?
» Don't be bothered by your lack of drawing skills, just do the best you can. Stick figures work fine!
» You can also work with a professional artist or visualiser who can visualise it in such a way that you can use it in your (external) communication.

A SOCIETY OF CURIOSITY

A foundation that offers a library, a kids' programme, theatre and music performances and that awards scientists and writers for their work was operating from a deep conviction that they should encourage artists and scientists who create culture and knowledge and make it accessible to all. Everyone on the team understands why they do what they do, but few people were able to put it into words in a way that they all agreed on or were inspired by. During a workshop session we first spoke about what they are fighting: a society where people are uneducated, kept ignorant, where dogmatic views rule and people are not creative or critical thinkers. Then we defined the opposite: a society of curiosity. We then imagined a city square, and what we would all like to see happening on it. We drew it out in a very basic sketch.
While we were drawing, the team came up with dozens of new ideas: 3-D printing hubs, co-working spaces, design programmes for children. This is the power of visualisation: now we can all see the future, we can all create ideas on how we can get there! The foundation will commission an artist to make the vision drawing clearer and plans to hang the work in their office, library and facilities and to include it in all their communications.

EXERCISE
MAKE YOUR MANIFESTO

A manifesto outlines your intentions and motivations. Writing a manifesto (with your team) and sharing it makes those intentions tangible and actionable.

WHAT IT'S FOR

» Articulating your intentions and motivations.
» Building the foundation for a strong organisational culture.
» Creating a movement of like-minded people.

HOW TO USE IT

» Make a list, either writing in stream-of-consciousness style or creating a mindmap.
» Work alone or co-create with a team.
» Ask yourself the following questions (plus any others you think of): What do you want to accomplish? What do you believe to be true? What is the driving force behind everything you work for? What kind of world do you want to live in?
» Select the most distinguishing and actionable elements and craft them into a half-page or one-page manifesto.
» Share your manifesto internally or externally.
» Keep it around as a reminder for yourself and others.

THE METHOD CLEANING HUMANIFESTO

We look at the world through bright-green coloured glasses.

We prefer ingredients that come from plants, not chemical plants.

We see that guinea pigs are never used as guinea pigs.

We're entranced by shiny objects, like clean dinner plates, floors you could eat off of, Nobel Peace Prizes and tasteful public sculptures.

We make role models in bottles.

We're the kind of people who've figured out that once you clean your home, a mess of other problems seem to disappear too.

We always see the scent glass as half full, and assume everyone we meet will smell like fresh cut grass or a similar yummy, nothing-but-good fragrance.

We exercise by running through the legs of the giant. Which is even more fun when a sprinkler is going.

We love a freshly detoxed home, we think perfect is boring, and weirdliness is next to godliness.

It's 'Everybody into the pool!'
(We believe in spontaneous bursts of enthusiasm.)

We also believe in making products safe for every surface, especially earth's.

We consider mistakes little messes we can learn from; nothing that can't be cleaned up and made better.

We embrace the golden ylang-ylang rule: do unto your home as you would do unto you. (Your shower doesn't want to have morning breath any more than you do.)

We believe above all else that dirty, in all its slime, smoggy, toxic, disgusting incarnations is public enemy number one. Good always prevails over stinky.

SUGRU'S FIXER'S MANIFESTO

1. If it's broken, fix it! Everyday practical problemsolving is a beautiful form of creativity, and just a little subversive.

2. If it's not broken, improve it. A tiny tweak can transform how something works for years to come.

3. And if it doesn't exist, make it. Everyone is inherently creative–even if we don't think we are.

4. Give your stuff a longer life. In a world that's full of waste, every fix counts.

5. Disposability is a choice. When we double the life of our things, we halve what goes to landfill.

6. Resist needless trends and upgrades. Fixing frees us from the tyranny of the new.

7. Embrace the stuff we already have. Let's use our imagination to keep it, use it, love it, fix it.

8. A fixed thing is a beautiful thing. Every fix tells a story.

9. Nurture curiosity. Anything can be learned by doing.

10. Share your ideas. With each fix, we build a global movement for positive change.

SHOW PERSONALITY

You can't write a manifesto without showing personality. Some people and organisations are very formal or diplomatic. Others are pragmatic. Some are radically outspoken. Great manifestos don't beat around the bush. Great manifestos have a tone of voice that becomes an unmistakable, inimitable part of the brand.

THE ACUMEN MANIFESTO

It starts by standing with the poor, listening to voices unheard, and recognising potential where others see despair.

It demands investing as a means, not an end, daring to go where markets have failed and aid has fallen short. It makes capital work for us, not control us.

It thrives on moral imagination: the humility to see the world as it is, and the audacity to imagine the world as it could be. It's having the ambition to learn at the edge, the wisdom to admit failure, and the courage to start again.

It requires patience and kindness, resilience and grit: a hard-edged hope. It's leadership that rejects complacency, breaks through bureaucracy, and challenges corruption. Doing what's right, not what's easy.

Acumen: it's the radical idea of creating hope in a cynical world. Changing the way the world tackles poverty and building a world based on dignity.

STANFORD D-SCHOOL ON A NAPKIN

Our intent: create the best design school. Period.

Prepare future innovators to be breakthrough thinkers and doers.

Use design thinking to inspire multidisciplinary teams.

Foster radical collaboration between students, faculty & industry.

Tackle big projects and use prototyping to discover new solutions.

EXERCISE
THE FRAME GAME

This exercise helps you and your team to play around with words to describe your offer and the value it holds.

WHAT IT'S FOR
» Clarifying your offer and its value.
» Teasing out compelling brand promises.

HOW TO USE IT
» Get your team together or ask several people who know what you do to join you.
» Grab a couple of objects that are unrelated to what you do: a soccer ball or a cup of coffee.
» Write the name or logo of your organisation, product or service on a piece of cardboard or nondescript box.
» Sit in a circle and pass around the first object.
» You pass the object around and each person finishes the following sentence: 'You are...'.
» Play a few rounds until you are out of ideas.
» Repeat the exercise but this time, finish the sentence: 'You could be...'
» Repeat the exercise with as many objects as you want in order to get your creative energy flowing.
» Now use the object that represents your service/product. Repeat the exercise as before.
» Be bold: there are no wrong answers!
» Make notes so you don't lose the ideas.

Write your product/service/organisation's name on a blank box or other nondescript item

ROUND ONE

You are my brother's best friend.
You are round.
You are white and black.
You are an object of desire across the world.
You are every child's favourite toy.
You are made in many different sizes.
You are potentially made through child labour.
You are made of rubber.

You could be therapy for a child who has seen too much.
You could be my friend if I had good hand-eye coordination.
You could be the ball that Ronaldo played with when he was young.
You could be deflatable so I can take you everywhere.
You could be bright orange so I can tell you apart from your colleagues.
You could be made of organic materials.

ROUND TWO

You are my saviour in the morning.
You are an addiction.
You are the reason my husband gets out of his grumpy moods in the morning.
You are from Guatemala.
You are grown by a farmer.
You are great in desserts too.
You are a commodity.
You are dark and delicious.
You smell so good!!

You could be less bitter.
You could be a way to earn a fair living for farmers.
You could have many flavours.
Your packaging could keep you fresher longer.
You could ensure I don't get bad breath and yellow teeth.
You could be a force for good.
You could wear way fewer clothes.

ROUND THREE

You are a job platform for people with disabilities.
You are a place to find a job.
You are a place to find motivated employees.
You are a place to find diverse additions to my team.
You are a quick & easy way to diversify my team.
You are a platform for talent without borders.
You are a place to find talent with extraordinary abilities.

You could be a solution to my challenge of staffing 5% of my team with people with disabilities.
You could be integrated into a regular job board.
You could be the place where I find people with unlimited motivation.
You could play a role in reframing how people think about employees with disabilities.
You could help people build a career without limits.

EXERCISE
THE BULLSHIT RADAR

Do you have a hard time describing what it is you do? Do you use a lot of jargon? Turn on your bullshit radar to ensure that what you say makes sense to your audiences.

WHAT IT'S FOR

» Clarifying your message.
» Getting through to your audiences.

HOW TO USE IT

» Ask a friend, family member, colleague, coach or potential client to join you in a ten-minute, one-on-one conversation.
» Record the conversation so you don't have to take notes.
» Stand opposite each other. Your conversational partner plays the role of bullshit radar.
» Tell them your vision, mission and/or some of your brand promises.
» Ask them to stop you mid-sentence when they don't understand, using only these phrases: 'Why?' 'How?' 'I don't know what that means.'
» Test different ways of phrasing what you do or why it matters. Play with words. Be wary of jargon. Try to be as specific as possible about what you do, for whom and/or why. Some phrases are used so often they can belong to hundreds of organisations.
» Draw lessons from the conversation to fine-tune your story.

* We have anonymised these statements for discretion's sake, but it's interesting to know they are real-world examples currently in use.

Factory45 takes sustainable apparel companies from idea to launch. We help you source fabric, find a manufacturer and raise money to fund production.

X* is involved in capacity building through arts. We believe creativity can save the world!

X* supports social entrepreneurs who are leading and collaborating with changemakers in a team-of-teams model that addresses the fluidity of a rapidly evolving society.

GoogleIdeas builds products to support free expression and access to information for people who need it most — those facing violence and harassment.

TribeWanted: Off-grid community tourism experiences in Africa, Asia & Europe.

We are X*, a sustainability crucible for cradle-to-cradle concepts and circle-economy research enabling environmental activists to empower communities.

 The mission of X* is to improve significantly the psychological, career, financial and legal well-being of women, men, couples and families, regardless of their ability to pay.

ClientEarth: We are activist lawyers committed to securing a healthy planet.

Peek Vision: Professional eye exams from your smartphone. With a mobile app and lens adapter we provide an easy-to-use, affordable and portable system for testing eyes, whether in a clinic or in the comfort of a patient's home.

EXERCISE
THE VALUES GAME

ROUND #1

- Get two or more colleagues together.
- Individually, write down six values you feel represent your organisation's driving beliefs on individual cards or sticky notes.
- Take turns presenting one chosen value with a short explanation: 'This value is important to us, because ...'

PRESENT TO THE GROUP

CHALLENGE!

ROUND #2

- Place the surviving values on the table.
- Vote on the values that you feel are the most fundamental with a show of hands. Each team member can vote for a maximum of three values.
- The six values (or fewer, if only those survived the challenge) with the most votes become your longlist.
- Co-create the definitions of the values.
- Each team member picks a definition to present to the group for the final challenge.

PRESENT TO THE GROUP

CHALLENGE!

ROUND #3

CAPTURE

- Place the surviving values on the table.
- Vote. Each team member can vote for three values maximum.
- The three values with the most votes win.
- Capture your results in a photo.
- Make a little book of values to distribute to colleagues, partners and external audiences.

Defining and living values as a team can be complex. Apply play!

WHAT IT'S FOR

» Sparking ideas.
» Discovering the values that truly guide your actions.
» To build ownership on values with your team.

HOW YOU USE IT

» Follow the line from 'Round' 1 to 'capture'.
» When a player presents their values, each of the other players can challenge him/her with a HOW question. For instance:

How does this value guide the way we hire staff, buy our source material, have lunch, make decisions about incoming opportunities, decide on partnerships, etc.

» Unchallenged values go on to the next round.
» Values that were picked by more than one player are merged as one proposal.
» If a value is challenged and the challenger is satisfied, the value can go on to the next round. When the challenger is not satisfied, the issue is resolved by a show of hands of the entire team.

EXERCISE
VISUAL BRANDING TESTS

Judging the strength of creative concepts for a visual identity is not easy if you are not experienced. You can get stuck on questions of taste or only focus on the communicative aspect. Visual performance is often overlooked although this is the embodiment of everything you do.

WHAT IT'S FOR
» Conducting a quick performance test.
» Finding ways to improve on the identity.

HOW TO USE IT
» Use the tests on creative concept proposals or to review your existing brand.

TEST #1 SIZE MATTERS
What would the logo look like on the top of a pen, the tail of an airplane or as the square thumbnail of an app? Is it iconic enough to perform on those scales? Is it still recognisable?

TEST #2 BEYOND THE LOGO
Take one of your brochures, newsletters or advertisements, or the visual design of your home page, and cover the logo. Is what is left still recognisable as you? Are you building an identity with a visual language that is so unique that it creates a recognisable brand, even if this brochure is right in the middle of a stack of other brochures, or even as I am flipping between sites and pages online?

TEST #3 COMPETITIVE ENVIRONMENT
Create a poster with an array of logos of other organisations (both collaborators and competitors) from your market. Make sure all the logos are about the same size and evenly spaced, with your logo (concept) placed in a random spot. Do you stand out? What do you have in common? Is there a visual space (a colour, a shape, a typeface) that has not been claimed yet?

TEST #4 THE WAR ROOM
Create a collage of your brand's interactions with your audiences, and do the same for the competition (or a brand you admire, used as a benchmark). Gather ads, brochures, flyers, home pages, Twitter and Facebook page headers, etc. Do you really stand out? Are you recognisably different?

EXERCISE
THE REPUTATION TURNAROUND

Sometimes our reputation is not what we want it to be and people recognise us for the wrong things, or not at all.

WHAT IT'S FOR

» Mapping out which actions build towards your desired reputation, and which detract from it.

» Creating an overview of what you need to do more of (or less of) in order to arrive at your desired reputation.

HOW TO USE IT

» Look at your present situation (A) and your target situation (B).

» Draw the model on the right on a large piece of paper or a whiteboard. Map out what you are currently doing that contributes to building state A, as well as what contributes to reaching state B.

» Stop or scale down everything that contributes to A. Start or scale up everything that contributes to B.

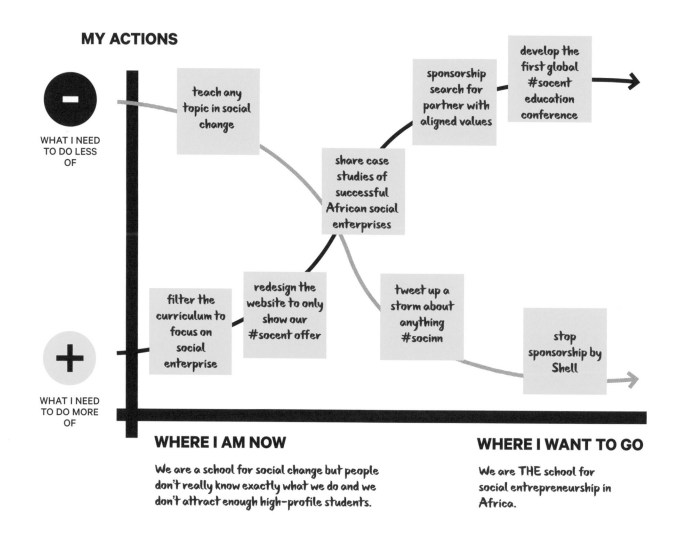

MY ACTIONS

WHAT I NEED TO DO LESS OF

WHAT I NEED TO DO MORE OF

teach any topic in social change

sponsorship search for partner with aligned values

develop the first global #socent education conference

share case studies of successful African social enterprises

filter the curriculum to focus on social enterprise

redesign the website to only show our #socent offer

tweet up a storm about anything #socinn

stop sponsorship by Shell

WHERE I AM NOW

We are a school for social change but people don't really know exactly what we do and we don't attract enough high-profile students.

WHERE I WANT TO GO

We are THE school for social entrepreneurship in Africa.

EXERCISE
BRAND REFRAMING

Are you looking for a new frame for your existing brand? Reframing can help you to successfully redefine your purpose, reputation or mission.

WHAT IT'S FOR

» Supporting a rebranding/repositioning or creating a new positive focus around a problem area.

HOW TO USE IT

1. Determine your core belief about the problem. Write it on a sticky note.
2. Map the beliefs that support the core belief on notes around it. Select the four most important ones and place them at the corners surrounding the core belief.
3. Find opposites for each of your supporting beliefs. Write them on sticky notes of a different colour and place them underneath the notes from Step 2. Make the opposites extreme; they don't even have to be realistic or possible.
4. Construct a reframed core belief from your findings in Step 3. You want to formulate it in such a way that you frame a solution to your defined problem from Step 1.

This tool appears courtesy of THNK, the School of Creative Leadership and Karim Benammar. Find the online reframing tool at reframe.thnk.org

EXAMPLE 1: MAURITIUS

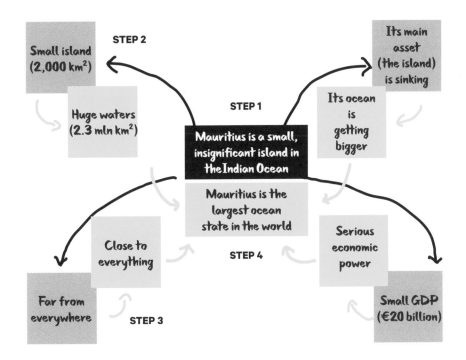

EXAMPLE 2:MINISTRY OF DEFENCE

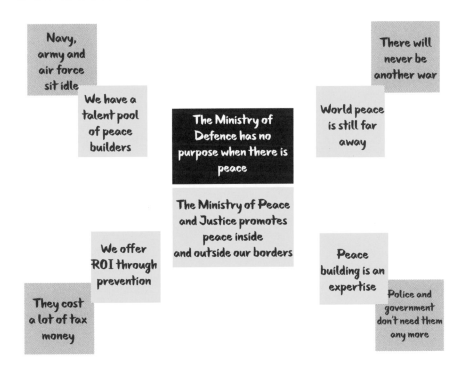

EXERCISE
BRAND
CHECKUP

Are you looking for a new frame for your existing brand? Reframing can help you to successfully redefine your purpose, reputation or mission.

WHAT IT'S FOR
» To check if your brand is ahead of the curve.
» To keep the brand fresh and relevant.

HOW TO USE IT
» Use the checklist every 6–12 months to see where you stand and to find out where there is room for improvement.
» Use it to do a broad check and use your team and audience as a sounding board. Certain points like checking insight and proposition could benefit from more in-depth market research.

TRENDS

Market trends, consumer trends, cultural trends all influence the relevance of your offer and the ways in which you interact with your audience. Keep up to date on these developments with trend reports, many of which can be found online for free or for a subscription fee.

1. BRAND INSIGHT Is the problem that you signalled in the world, or the need that you observed on which you built your offer, still relevant? It is possible you or other players have significantly addressed it or that circumstances have changed.   ○ yes   ○ no

2. BRAND PROPOSITION Is the proposition you offer still a compelling solution to the problem or need? Your proposition can be challenged by technological advances, trends, a competitor offering similar or better products/services, etc. If it is not a compelling solution, adapt it.   ○ yes   ○ no

3. BRAND CORE: VISION AND MISSION After 6–12 months of sharing your vision and mission and using them as a guiding force for your brand, do you, your team and your audiences find it inspiring and does it offer a clear direction for the future? If not, fine-tune or reframe it.   ○ yes   ○ no

4. BRAND CORE: VALUES Are you living your values? If you are not, brainstorm where in the six types of brand interactions* you can improve the integration of your values.   ○ yes   ○ no

5. BRAND CORE: BRAND PROMISES Are you delivering on your promises? If so, brainstorm how can you take your brand promises one step further. If not, improve delivery.   ○ yes   ○ no

6. BRAND IDENTITY: VISUAL What does your competitive field look like and do you still stand out from the crowd? Is your visual identity strong, distinctive and consistent?   ○ yes   ○ no

7. BRAND IDENTITY: VERBAL Do you have a distinct tone of voice and does it appeal to your audience? Do you have a clear point of view and are your communications consistently communicating it?   ○ yes   ○ no

8. BRAND INTERACTIONS Have you been able to translate your brand to the outside world through all the available brand interactions*? Are they at the level of quality that you would like them to be?   ○ yes   ○ no

9. BRAND INTERACTIONS: COMMUNICATION Is your brand consistently implemented across media (off/online)? Are you communicating frequently with your audience to get and stay on their radar?   ○ yes   ○ no

10. AUDIENCES Do you have a clear understanding of your primary and secondary brand audiences? Is your communication reaching and engaging them? Are you building brand ambassadors and/or a community around your cause?   ○ yes   ○ no

CHAPTER 7
EXPERT TIPS AND TRICKS

Telling stories

ROSHAN PAUL

How a story can create an emotional connection between you and your audiences.

Roshan Paul is the co-founder and CEO of Amani Institute, based in Nairobi, São Paulo and Bangalore. Amani Institute provides new models of higher education that develops talent to solve 21st-century problems. Roshan holds a master's in Public Policy from the Harvard Kennedy School, was a Senior Change Manager at Ashoka, writes frequently for the Stanford Social Innovation Review, and published his first novel in 2014.

Strong brands thrive on storytelling. An emotional, personal narrative of a founder, a team or a client, can be far more impactful in building a tribe of followers than traditional, analytical communication. A good story creates an emotional connection between you and your audiences, allowing them to remember it, identify with it, and share it with others.

As a master's student at Harvard University in the early days of Barack Obama's unlikely run for president, I had the incredible luck to work with Marshall Ganz, who had developed a technique for telling stories in ways that moved people to act. Ganz applied his technique, based on over 30 years of working in community organising across the United States, to the Obama campaign with transformative effect. He has been credited as the mastermind behind the campaign strategy that led to the record voter turnout that ushered in America's first black president.

If you have heard of the importance of storytelling as a professional skill any time in the last decade, chances are the trail leads back to the Obama campaign and to Marshall Ganz. His propagation of the tool, through his students' subsequent work (mine included), has spawned an industry of books, TED Talks, consulting firms, and professional story coaches. So what's all the fuss about? How do stories work?

As Marshall writes, human beings interpret the world in two ways: through analysis and through narrative. Analysis uses critical reasoning, data and deliberation to teach us how to act. Narrative uses story and emotion to teach us how we feel about things, which in turn tells us why we act.

Unfortunately, in most of our professional communication we use analysis to persuade others, despite mounting evidence that people are more effectively moved by stories. When it comes to getting people to act, the most brilliant piece of analytical reasoning is simply no match for the specific, well-told, detail-filled story.

Take, for instance, Acumen founder Jacqueline Novogratz. To demonstrate the interconnectedness of humanity in today's globalised world (and thus our obligation to help others less fortunate), she could present an economic analysis about international trade and flows of goods and services.

Nobody would remember a word of it.

Instead she tells the story of her blue sweater. The sweater, which pictured zebras grazing in front of Mount Kilimanjaro, was Novogratz's most beloved piece of clothing throughout middle school. After a ninth-grade classmate made fun of Novogratz for wearing the now ill-fitting sweater during high school, Novogratz donated it to charity. Fast-forward ten years: Novogratz is working in Rwanda when she sees a young boy wearing the exact same sweater. She runs over to him and looks at the sweater's tag. Sure enough, her name is there, in faded black ink.

This story makes the same point about the interconnectedness of humanity in a modern economy as a presentation on trade flows would, but it does so better. Like Novogratz's name in faded black ink on the sweater's tag, the story leaves an indelible image in our minds. We remember it.

What are the principles of great storytelling, particularly that which makes a request of its audience to act on something? Here are three guiding principles, which you can use to underpin your pitches, presentations, media interviews and even personal conversations.

1 PUT YOURSELF IN THE STORY: SHOW WHY YOU ARE DOING IT.

As Simon Sinek famously argued in his viral TEDx Talk, 'People don't buy what you do, they buy why you do it'. Many people hesitate to talk about themselves or their motivations, but without that information, nobody will follow you because they don't understand clearly why what you're doing matters to you. And very pragmatically, when people don't understand you, they make up a story about you anyway. It's how the human mind works. So why not proactively give them the story they need to understand you?

2 SHOW THE AUDIENCE WHY THEY SHOULD CARE: CONNECT WITH THEIR VALUES.

We take action based on our emotions, which in turn are driven by our values. We rarely act based on intellectual understanding. For effective leadership, you must connect with what the audience already believes about itself. Nothing moves us more to act than when we feel threatened or inspired or compassionate or empowered, all emotions that are at the heart of taking action. This is the hard part of storytelling, where you help the audience understand what's in it for them.

3 HELP THEM KNOW WHAT TO DO: MAKE A SPECIFIC CALL TO ACTION.

When you make the ask, it's critical that you ask the audience to do something specific. There is a huge difference between a generic 'Support Syrian refugees' or 'Join my gay rights campaign' call to action and a highly specific 'Go to X website right now and make a donation to Y organisation's refugee camps in Jordan' or 'Attend Saturday's rally in front of Parliament to protest recent legislation against LGBT+ people'. The first examples don't give the audience a clear idea of how to act; the second ones do.

Use your story to build your brand. Put yourself in the story (i.e. why you're doing it), show the audience why they should care (i.e. why join you), and help them know what to do.

Find Roshan Paul at
amaniinstitute.org
@roshpaul

Getting publicity
SIMON BUCKBY

How to get positive coverage in relevant media outlets to catalyse your brand.

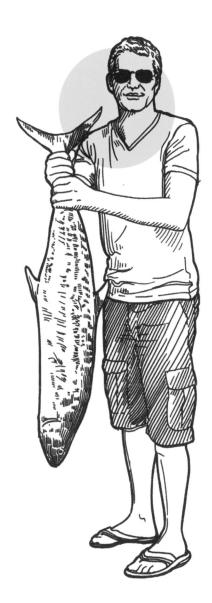

Simon Buckby is a former journalist for the *Financial Times* and the BBC. Twelve years ago, he founded Champollion, a London-based independent communications consultancy specialising in media relations, public affairs and digital channels.

Though press is often called free publicity, it is hard-earned. It requires smart strategy, great stories, and a time investment to get journalists to take notice. No matter where you are in the world, no matter which outlet you want to appear in, there are common rules about how to play the media game, rules that most social entrepreneurs haven't had the time to learn. Yet they are rules that you can easily learn so you can start playing on a level surface.

First and foremost, it is a mistake to think that spreading your messages far and wide is the way to generate interest.

WHEN I WAS A JOURNALIST, I RECEIVED LITERALLY DOZENS OF PRESS RELEASES EVERY DAY

I had no idea who they were from or what they were about. I certainly didn't have the time to look at them, because that's not how most journalists get their stories.

TARGET SPECIFICALLY
Far better than this scattergun approach is to target specifically. You shouldn't be trawling aimlessly in the deep sea for random fish by pumping out press releases or randomly firing off tweets; you are trying to catch a few prize specimens which hang out in particular places.

IDENTIFY MEDIA OUTLETS
The starting point should be to identify which media outlets really are the most important to you. Who are you ultimately trying to reach? What media do they consume? Is it a particular trade publication or webzine?

IDENTIFY THE JOURNALIST
Once you know where you want to appear, you should be clear about which journalists on those outlets are most likely to cover your sort of story, especially from a sympathetic point of view.

That means you have to read their stuff. There is nothing more off-putting than being pitched a story by someone who has quite obviously never read a word that you have written.

BECOME A RELIABLE SOURCE

Then you need to make sure you have stories that are actually of potential interest to those journalists. It is so common to be contacted by press officers who have something that is really only of concern to that organisation and nobody else at all in the outside world.

WHAT JOURNALISTS NEED ARE RELIABLE SOURCES, PEOPLE WHO WILL GIVE THEM MATERIAL THAT THEY CAN COVER, THAT MAKES THEM LOOK GOOD

Not just once, but again and again. There are two crucial criteria for becoming such a source.

BE CREDIBLE

First, you need to have credibility on the matter in hand. If you are working with older people, then you need to draw on that experience to give you the right to have your views heard about issues affecting older people. Second, once you are credible, you need to have something to say that adds value to the known stock of information. A piece of data. A line of argument. An insight. New news. Something that moves the story forward. Put these two together and you have a fighting chance of getting some coverage. All you have to do then is get your execution right.

OFFER SOMETHING OF VALUE

Journalists don't need people who want something from them. They need people who are offering them something. And the way to show you are one of the latter, not the former, is to try to nurture long-term relationships with a small number of your targets. Reach out to them directly and show that you are interested in their work and can contribute to it. Write positive letters about their articles to the editor of their publication. Send them emails saying you really enjoyed watching a piece of their coverage. Tweet them directly. Comment supportively on their blogs and web feeds. Don't be weird and stalk them, but be just active enough so that they know you are trying to get to know them.

SHARE YOUR STORY

Then you can approach them –preferably by phone– to talk to them about your story idea. Ideally, show them that this idea is just for them, not for their rivals as well. And, as in most cases you are very unlikely to care whether it is published next week or next month as long as it looks good, why not ask the journalist when the most suitable time is for them, for the piece to be published?

This kind of flexible, supportive approach is far more likely to succeed. Not just at getting your first story to work, but more importantly to build a long-term relationship that means you can keep going back to each other for a long time to come. They are likely to be in their job for years to come, and hopefully so are you.

PR gets a bad name, not least because there are a lot of people who don't know what they are doing. But with just a bit of thought and maybe some short-term professional support to get you going, you can learn pretty quickly that you are not trying to net a load of small fish but to focus on building long-term relationships with a few bigger ones that might really matter to your brand.

Find Simon Buckby at
champollion.co.uk

Going to market

GRANT TUDOR

How marketing drives impact by better understanding, engaging and benefiting your users.

Marketing is the process by which an enterprise brings its value to market. For private firms, we know its capabilities are powerful. At Populist, we believe the same is true for social enterprises. Tasked with bringing value to some of the world's most marginalised groups, social enterprises can wield marketing to better serve customers and ultimately drive more impact.

Below is an introductory marketing process, five general steps –or rather, five big questions– to move through when asked, 'How might we increase our impact?' Taken together, they will set your organisation up to more effectively make use of marketing, and in turn bring more value to users.

1 WHAT'S OUR AMBITION?

Start with an intended result. What's the organisation's goal this year? How does it intend to impact its users? If you're bringing some product or service to market, this is usually straightforward: you likely either want more people adopting your offering, or people using it with more frequency.

If a social enterprise is selling clean cook stoves, for example, it might be concerned with market penetration, converting some number of people who use kerosene to its alternative product. Articulated, the ambition could read, 'an X per cent increase in cook stove sales, and a Y per cent decrease in kerosene use'.

An ambition should directly relate to impact: higher penetration means cleaner energy, healthier homes, and so on. To ensure measurability, it should also be quantitative. Your ambition will frame all subsequent activities, so make sure it's a wickedly clear and direct imperative.

2 WHAT'S OUR CONTEXT?

Your ambition won't live in a vacuum. It's bound to be affected by external forces. After setting a clear ambition, take the time to audit your context. Who's your direct and indirect competition, and what are they up to? What trends in your category might impact upon your efforts and those of your competition? For example, maybe the price of kerosene is falling, something bound to complicate cook stove sales.

One helpful way to think about an audit is to break it up into discrete market factors:
- Competition, or the alternative options available to various user groups.
- Category, or the type of market you're working in and its trends.
- Channels, or the delivery options for your offering, and how they might be changing.
- Consumers, or the various types of user segments engaging with you, with others, or perhaps with no one yet.
- Company, or the 'stuff' happening inside your own organisation that might support or detract from achieving your ambition.

This exercise will provide a clearer picture of your operating environment, its universe of user segments, and the preparedness of your enterprise. It should rid you of blinders as you start moving towards an ambition.

3 WHAT'S STANDING IN OUR WAY?

By implication, an ambition faces barriers. What's preventing people from engaging with what you're providing? What are they doing now, and what would you like them to be doing?

To find out, we conduct user research, the process of unpacking the many ways that people think, feel and behave, and properly identifying the variables shaping those thoughts, feelings and behaviours. It's arguably the hardest and most important part of the marketing process; without clear insights, marketing becomes an expensive guessing game.

There are, of course, many methodologies available to researchers. Quantitative tools like survey instruments are popular, and for good reason. Having people answer standardised questions allows for larger-scale and comparative results. These methods can also be limiting, however. Perhaps cook stove customers report in a survey that they use the product Monday through Friday, but they use kerosene during the weekend. Quantitative research did a good job of identifying a use pattern. But why? What explains that observation?

Qualitative methodologies, from observational research to individual interviews, help to probe at the determinants of behaviours. They're often better equipped to give us a more nuanced appreciation of people's feelings and behaviours. Ultimately, nothing replaces spending actual time with the people you're intending to impact upon.

User research should seek to both identify and explain the variables encouraging or preventing people from engaging with your offering. The result is a set of insights.

4 HOW DO WE RESPOND?

Armed with insights, the organisation is in a position to respond. Given what we know about users, how can we influence their environments and behaviours to support our ultimate ambition?

Take our fictional cook stove enterprise. Maybe user research found that many kerosene users want to switch to cook stoves, but the upfront cost is just too much. How might a payment plan change that? Or maybe people are plenty capable of paying for the cook stoves, but frankly, the products are ugly. How might we spruce them up? Or perhaps this new offering just isn't trusted to work. Strong brands can do a good job of building associations, like 'trusted'. Investing in your brand through advertising, then, might be the smart response. The suite of potential solutions to the issues surfaced by research is vast, from pricing strategies and packaging design, to product functions and advertising. This is marketing's creative process: generating ideas, designing mock-ups and testing them out.

5 HOW DO WE MEASURE OUR RESPONSE?

Creative ideas are ideas that work. Developing key performance indicators for creative ideas ensures that you're measuring progress. The methodologies available to marketeers for evaluating, iterating and improving ideas are abundant. Quantitative evaluators –say, net adoption of those payment plans– are helpful for tracking progress. They can determine whether you're positioned to meet objectives. But qualitative research helps you to iterate ideas, not just track them. Maybe

people are asking about that payment plan, but aren't following through. What might user interviews reveal? Continuous enquiry helps to tweak and improve ideas over time. Measurement should be an exercise in always-on user research.

Taken together, these activities comprise a fuller function for marketing inside your organisation. Marketing isn't about expensive ads or about pithy taglines. It's the systemic process of driving more impact with user-centric activities. It offers those in the business of serving others a way to serve better.

Your marketing plan must focus on reaching your organisation's specific goals and generating measurable results. Marketing need not be expensive, flashy or clever. Your marketing strategy must be based on insight into the real-world needs and desires of your customers.

Find Grant Tudor at
populistgroup.org
@g_tudor

Grant Tudor is the founder and CEO of Populist, a not-for-profit marketing group helping social enterprises sell vital products and services to marginalised and underserved populations.

Protecting your brand
MARLEEN SPLINTER

How a trademarked brand protects you from costly challenges by copycats or competitors, increasing the value of your enterprise.

Marleen Splinter is the co-founder of Rise Brands, a law firm specialising in trademarking brands. Her mission is to protect her clients' brands and ensure that they can grow and thrive without legal conflicts that could limit their opportunities.

You are building your brand and things could not be more exciting right now. Trademark protection is probably the last thing on your mind, but you must think about protecting your brand now or risk serious trouble down the line. A forced rebranding is a terrible loss of name recognition, financial investment and time.

Why trademark your brand?
- It gives you a certain degree of security about your right to use the trademark.
- It enables you to act when someone else copies your trademark.
- It increases the value of your company when you sell it or increase shares.
- It enables you to attract investors.
- Most importantly, a proper trademark portfolio prevents problems and conflicts with other trademarks.

WHAT IS A TRADEMARK?
A trademark is a distinctive sign that enables consumers to identify your organisation, product or service. A word, logo, shape, song, slogan or a combination of these can all be trademarks. Strong trademarks are signs that are very distinctive and don't cause any confusion or association with other existing brands.

THE PROCEDURE
Entering your company in a business register and registering your website domain are important, but neither will ensure you any trademark rights. Your brand will be legally protected by trademark law only once you have registered your trademark. In most countries this is achieved through an administrative procedure.

1 FIND OUT IF YOUR NAME CAN BE REGISTERED
Ensure your brand name can be registered and is available in the countries where you plan to operate. Only distinctive trademarks can be registered. If your brand name is generic or strictly descriptive, it cannot be registered as a trademark.

Examples of non-registrable words:
- SUPER for insurance products (or any other product).
- CHEESE for a cheese snack.
- BIKEFACTORY for a bicycle shop.

You would need to add a distinguishing element to enable a registration but the scope of protection remains very limited.

Examples of (initially) weak, but registrable trademarks:
- HELTTI for healthy food products.
- PINTEREST for online curating of digital media.
- LINKEDIN for an online network of professional people.

These brands can be protected as a trademark, but can only be invoked against practically identical trademarks.

Examples of strong trademarks:
- GILLETTE for shaving products.
- APPLE for computers.
- TWITTER for an online instant messaging service.

The stronger the brand, the broader the trademark protection.

FIND OUT IF YOUR TRADEMARK IS AVAILABLE

A brand should be unique and not cause confusion with other brands so that the consumer will be able to distinguish your brand from others in the market. If you are looking for new glasses of a certain brand, you will not be confused if you find a brand of milk with the same name. A somewhat similar trademark for identical products might, however, cause confusion.

An availability search* can determine the risk of conflicts and objections. You can do an initial assessment of the availability of a trademark yourself by searching the trademark registers in the relevant territory for the relevant classes, by searching the Internet and by searching domain name registers and social media accounts. Clearing a brand with a high degree of certainty is work for professionals; ask professional advice!

DETERMINE WHAT YOU WILL REGISTER

Word mark or combined word-device mark? It is preferable to register a word mark, unless the word is not sufficiently distinctive, in which case you can register a word-logo combination. Be aware that if you register a word-logo combination, any changes to the logo will require you to apply for a new trademark registration, which involves high costs and loss of prior rights. *What products/classification?* Trademark rights are valid for specific product types, therefore the application of a trademark must identify the goods and services the protection is claimed for. It is not possible to change the registration afterwards, so it's essential to formulate an accurate description of your current and future activities. Especially in the case of a new product which has not been described before, this can be quite complicated. In case of doubt, contact a professional. The classification you use will determine the extent of the protection of your trademark.

REGISTER YOUR TRADEMARK AT HOME AND ABROAD

Registering your brand in one territory does not guarantee freedom to operate in other territories. For instance: Skype was introduced in 2003 but the EU trademark application of the brand recently encountered a major obstacle because of the prior trademark 'SKY' owned by a UK company. Pinterest is trademarked and used broadly in the US, but the EU trademark filing was blocked because of a prior identical trademark in the EU.

It is wise to register your trademark in each country where you are active, but an occasional client abroad might not justify the costs of a trademark registration. A good trademark portfolio must support your business, so consider the expense in relation to your actual interest in obtaining trademark protection. If you have sufficient resources, you can choose to trademark your brand proactively, but remember that in most countries you must use your trademark within three or five years, so it is not possible to reserve a trademark indefinitely.

A trademark conflict can put your brand out of business, so take trademarking seriously.

Find Marleen Splinter at
risemerken.nl
@RiseMerken

* Find a list of online resources in the back of this book.

Selling sustainability
STELLA VAN HIMBERGEN

How to make sustainability a selling point for your target audience.

There is an increasing demand for products and services that are greener, healthier, better priced and more convenient. In this scenario, sustainability sounds like a no-brainer. However, consumers are less rational than we think. As a result, many companies offering sustainable products aren't sure how to make sustainability a part of their story. Not every consumer responds to sustainability arguments in the same way. If you want to build a brand and grow your customer base, it is crucial to dive into the world of your audience.

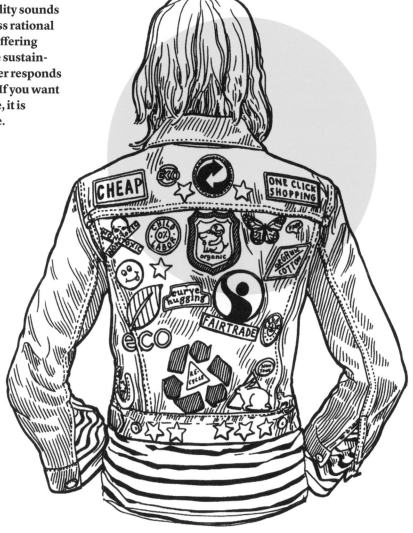

Stella van Himbergen is the CEO of Dutch Design in Development, which helps companies create sustainable products through strategy development, consultancy, training and sourcing of designers and producers.

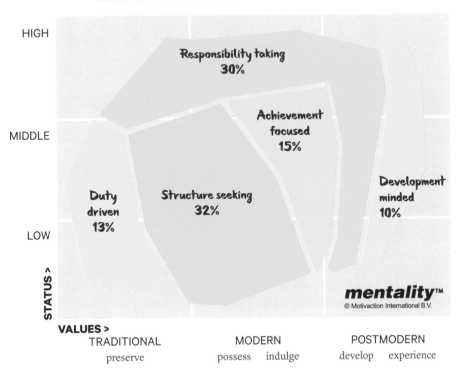

SUSTAINABILITY SEGMENTATION FOR THE NETHERLANDS

Figure labels:

STATUS > : HIGH, MIDDLE, LOW

Responsibility taking 30%

Achievement focused 15%

Development minded 10%

Duty driven 13%

Structure seeking 32%

mentality™
© Motivaction International B.V.

VALUES >
TRADITIONAL — preserve
MODERN — possess, indulge
POSTMODERN — develop, experience

EXAMPLE: THE NETHERLANDS

To give you an idea of what these segmentations can look like, let's take the Netherlands as an example. According to Motivaction, people look at sustainability in roughly five different ways (see model).

A closer look at two of these groups will help to illustrate how groups differ in mindset and how you need to approach them in order to create a connection.

'Structure Seeking' people form the biggest group. They are materialistic and enjoy life. Sustainability to them is a vague concept and is only interesting when it is cheap. If you want to reach this group, you need to understand that purchasing the product should be easy and the costs low.

'Development Minded' people form another group. They are prepared to pay more for sustainable products but won't go out of their way to find them. This group does not like to be coddled in communication. They do their own thing and will switch to sustainable when it is personally relevant and super convenient. Part of this group thinks a sustainable lifestyle is 'trendy'.

Segment sizes are constantly changing. For instance, the group 'Achievement Focused' (15%) will grow to 20% in the near future.

Generating consumer interest in sustainable products is a complicated endeavour. In general, people are concerned with things that touch their daily life. It is far easier to connect with people on sustainable food than it is on fair fashion. A pair of jeans produced under awful circumstances in Bangladesh has less of an impact on the life of a consumer than a health claim by a chocolate brand. And even when people care, they still need to turn their good intentions into purchases. You need people who are not just concerned with the environment, but are willing to get rid of their car and start using your car sharing service.

A GROWING AUDIENCE

The group of people interested in sustainability is growing, and knowing their different motivations can be the key to success in sales. Some people can be enticed when a sustainable product is cheaper, others when they see their sense of status or self-worth rise by using a product. To map out these audiences and their motivations, entrepreneurs often turn to market research agencies who use lifestyle segmentation to get a better insight into potential groups of customers.

Researchers categorise societal and consumer groups based on variables such as age, income, education, family situation and life phase. These factors are connected to attitude, behaviour, opinion, intention and consumption patterns. Every country or market has its own segments. Knowing the audiences in your market helps you to influence their beliefs and move them to act.

The Dutch market research agency Motivaction has defined a model that works for Western, affluent countries. Motivaction and Sinus (a German agency) also have models adapted to Eastern Europe and Asia.

CHECK IF THERE IS AVAILABLE RESEARCH FOR YOUR MARKETS

If nothing is available, consider hiring a market research agency to do the research for you.

Knowing your market, the consumer attitudes towards and beliefs on a certain topic (whether it is car sharing, fair trade jeans or organic, slave-free chocolate), helps you to find the arguments and tone of voice that hit the right chord. There is no 'one right way' to this process, but the following roadmap can help you as you go.

DEFINE YOUR TARGET GROUP

Who will you aim for? Start with a standard social demographic group. It may be based on age, sex or family situation, for example. It may be geographical, located in a city, a region or a country. Socio-demographic data is often available for free through government agencies.

RESEARCH THE MARKET

What is its size? What are the most important developments? What is the competition doing? How is their product positioned or priced? This data is often readily available through market research agencies.

DEFINE THE VALUE AND LIFESTYLE YOU AIM FOR

Zoom in on the values your target group is sensitive to. What exemplifies their mentality? What are the considerations that come into play when it comes to their sustainable behaviour?

DEFINE A TONE OF COMMUNICATIONS FOR THE TARGET GROUP

Do you want to sound playful? Down-to-earth? Sophisticated? Make sure your tone resonates with the values and the lifestyle profile of your target group.

5 CO-CREATE A VALUE PROPOSITION

Involve your target group in your qualitative research, the initiatives you develop and your communications by organising in-depth interviews or group discussions. Check if your approach fits with them.

6 MEASURE THE IMPACT

Review with your target audience whether the approach has had the right effect. If necessary, adjust.

Sustainability is not the defining element of a consumer's decision to buy your products. It's all about finding the right keys and motivations of the different consumer groups to make your brand a success.

Understanding the relationship between sustainability, consumer behaviour and branding is crucial to your success.

Find Stella van Himbergen at www.ddid.nl

SAINT BASICS

Saint Basics is a sustainable brand focused on selling stylish organic cotton underwear. Their brand story is 'It's easy to be a saint. Every time you wear Saint Basics, you automatically make the world a little more beautiful and a little more fair. And you look great while doing it! Together we make the difference, from the bottom up!' Saint Basics is focused on the new conservatives, the cosmopolitans and the social climbers and is successful with these groups.
They wanted to reach the postmodern hedonists, who are more cultural and creative, but this group felt that the Saint Basics collection was a little too basic. Based on these findings, Saint Basics developed a collection with more colour. The biggest group, the Structure Seekers, are hard to reach, due to the price range.

Going digital
BEN MATTHEWS

How to get the basics of digital marketing right.

Ben Matthews is a director at Montfort, a London-based digital marketing agency for people who change the world for good.

Digital marketing is the term for any activity that promotes your cause online. It covers everything from a blog post, to a tweet, a YouTube video to an advert on Google. This includes how people consume your marketing content–on a laptop, mobile or other device.

As more and more people get online, digital marketing has become increasingly important. In fact, many organisations now think 'digital first'. They market themselves online first, then think about how to promote themselves offline.

The lines between marketing online and offline have become blurred. Events that happen in the real world are captured, posted online and shared through social media. The online conversation around an issue then informs what happens offline, so it goes full circle. That's why we are seeing organisations lose the term 'digital' from their marketing. But they make sure that their offline and online activity is working together.

The wide range and low cost of digital tools and advertising makes digital marketing a great way to find and connect with your audience. It takes fewer resources than ever to get started and get noticed, but the large range of options available can make it difficult to know where to start.

Given the wide availability of digital marketing channels, how do you apply your limited resources to the online channels that will work for you?

Here's a step-by-step of priorities to follow that will get you on the right path to excel in digital marketing.

1 CONCENTRATE ON YOUR OWN WEBSITE FIRST
Your website is the main place that people will find out more about your organisation. It's here that people will read about what you do, why you do it and how to get involved. That's why before you do anything you should have a website in place.

If you do not have the budget available to hire a professional website designer, there are plenty of free website creators out there that will help you get a simple but effective website up and running. Take a look at Wordpress.com, or Striking.ly, as these services will give you a modern website for free.

As mobile usage increases globally, it's important that your website can be easily viewed and interacted with on mobile phones ('mobile-optimised'). This means that it has to load quickly in areas with slow mobile coverage, and work on feature phones as well as smartphones. Think text first and don't post large images onto your site-reduce the size of your photos to around 100Kb before uploading to your website.

ACTIONS
Build your organisation's website; make sure it loads quickly and is optimised for mobile devices

2 WRITE AS MUCH ABOUT YOUR AREA AS POSSIBLE
Most of the people who find your website will come from a search engine, like Google or Bing. For your website to show up in search results, you need to be writing about your topic area so that those search engines know what your website is about. This means publishing lots of text-based content to your website.

The more you publish to your website, the more the search engines can see your site and the more traffic you'll get. This can be 'about' pages, frequently asked question (FAQs) pages, team pages, etc.-or blog posts. By concentrating on your own website, you will be less reliant on other services. It is increasingly hard to get your content seen on, for instance, Facebook-even by your own fans. Building up your own website means you're more visible on search engines and get more reliable traffic than through social media.

ACTIONS
Based on your brand and what you want to be recognised for, consider your audience and which of their information needs you could write about, use as part of a blog, or as more content for you to publish on your website.

3 TAKE PHOTOS WHENEVER YOU CAN
An essential activity that will help your digital marketing is to take photos of your organisation as it goes about its everyday work. A picture paints a thousand words. Photos are the easiest way to show what exactly it is your organisation does, who you help and the impact you create.

Create a list of your events and activities. Identify if you have existing photos that capture these moments, or if you need to create more photos. Once you know what photos you need to get, either work with a photographer or encourage your team to take photos when they are doing their work. Your photos don't have to be perfect; it's better to capture the photos when you can, rather than miss an opportunity. Now you have photos, you have lots more content to share on your website and to post to social media.

ACTIONS
Create a checklist of events and activities and an archive of photos from your organisation's work, encourage your team to take on a reporter's mindset and share the photos online.

BEN'S ONLINE RESOURCES

There are some great guides for how you can use Facebook for business at facebook.com/business

Facebook has some excellent training resources for advertising at facebook.com/blueprint–take a look at these courses before starting your ad campaigns and you'll be off to a much better start.

This is a great list of how you can use Twitter for business: twitter.com/basics

For more help on using social video, download the Montfort guide to video at montfort.io/social-media-video/

4

THINK ABOUT SOCIAL VIDEO

In 2016, video posts on social media had a whopping 135% more organic reach than those without video. Social video can offer incredibly high ROI and be produced cost-effectively from scratch, or simply adapted from existing video.

The absolute best way to save yourself money (and time) is to repurpose and recycle the existing video in your archives. Are there any longer videos that you could slice up into shorter 15- or 30-second clips? Can you succinctly help illustrate your brand or campaign story by taking a small piece of a longer video and sharing it on Instagram, Twitter or Facebook?

Lastly, have you tried Facebook Live for your brand yet? If not, you should. Facebook Live is picking up.

The subject matter and real-time interactive element is what appeals to people watching a Facebook Live video, not the backdrop. So there's no need to worry if your budget is limited and it doesn't matter what sort of resources you have available: you can make it work and you should still be experimenting with Facebook Live.

ACTIONS

Find out what video content your organisation has that can be reused for social media; experiment with Facebook Live.

5

USE ORGANIC SOCIAL MEDIA TO BUILD AN AUDIENCE

Facebook and Twitter have a vast number of people using their platforms every day. You probably use at least one of these social networks and are used to how they work so it makes sense to have a presence there.

To build an audience and keep your fans engaged, you need to be posting to your Facebook page often: aim to post at least two to three times a week–more if you can manage it.

What you post doesn't have to be your own content. It can come from a news site or be a YouTube video. Post interesting, engaging or fun content that your fans will be interested in.

Twitter has fewer people using it than Facebook, but it is more

of a specialist platform. Twitter is great for reaching journalists, politicians, activists and other influencers that are relevant to your cause. Make sure to follow people relevant in your area, so that they can see you are following them and find out more about you.

Make sure you plan what content you are going to post. Rather than posting whatever comes to mind, focus on a few areas that are directly relevant to your cause. You'll be able to find content much more easily in that area and your fans and followers will know what to expect from your profiles.

6

USE PAID ADVERTISING TO DRIVE MORE TRAFFIC

If you're struggling to get traffic to your website, then paid advertising can help. Facebook offers the best value and best targeting options at the moment, but it's also worth looking at Google AdWords and Twitter Ads. Start with a small budget, say $100 per month, then expand as you get more confident in what is working for you.

Test variations in ads: Does Facebook work better than Google? Do video ads work better than images? What photo and copy combinations work best? Run several ads against each other to test and learn what works.

ACTION

Take the beginners Facebook Blueprint courses; experiment with ads using a small budget.

There's lots more we can get into around digital marketing, including email marketing, SEO and paid media. But concentrate on these basics first and you'll be off to a flying start with digital marketing.

Find Ben Matthews at
montfort.io
@benrmatthews
@montfortio

Building a brand architecture

SUZANNE VAN GOMPEL

How to manage the branding of a portfolio of products and services within one organisation

Suzanne van Gompel is a brand developer and director based in Bombay. In the last 20 years she has helped businesses in a broad range of markets to develop, (re)shape and establish their brands; from corporates to startups to charities. Currently she works via her own brand consultancy practice Stand Out From The Crowd.

When growing your business and expanding into new services or products, inevitably the question will arise: 'Do we need to create a new brand for this?'. Managing multiple brands is resource draining and should be considered from all angles before any decisions are made.

Say you've put your first brand successfully on the market, and your business is growing. Meanwhile, you've created an awesome new product or service. Should you launch it under the umbrella of your existing brand, or would it make more sense to develop a new brand? It goes without saying that the risks, costs and (expected) profits of developing a new brand are something you have to weigh carefully.

IT IS A MATTER OF DECIDING HOW MANY BRANDS YOU NEED VERSUS HOW MANY BRANDS YOU CAN FEED

In general, the answer to the question 'Should I launch a new brand?' is: 'No' unless one of the following situations applies:

1 YOU HAVE WHAT IT TAKES TO MAKE ANOTHER BRAND TAKE OFF

Creating a new brand is one thing. Getting and keeping it on customers' radar is quite another; it takes a lot of time, money and perseverance. The more limited your resources (budget, knowledgeable staff, time), the less advisable it is to launch a new brand.

2 YOUR CURRENT BRAND IS NOT CREDIBLE IN THE NEW MARKET SEGMENT/CATEGORY

McPizza might have sounded logical to the marketeers at McDonald's ('fast food is fast food'), but consumers preferred trusted, specialised pizzerias over burger joints. When Bic ('disposable products') launched disposable underwear, it flopped. The idea of buying intimate wear from a company that is known for pens failed to appeal to consumers.

3 YOUR NEW PRODUCT SOMEHOW CONFLICTS WITH YOUR CURRENT BRAND

Harley-Davidson motorcycles ('rebellious lifestyle') damaged their credibility when they introduced a line of wine coolers in the mid-1980s. Hells Angels sipping wine? When Nivea ('trusted skincare') launched a makeup line it became a flop. In Nivea customers' eyes, makeup and skincare were incompatible.

4 THE (PRICE) POSITIONING OF YOUR EXISTING AND NEW PRODUCT ARE NOT COMPATIBLE

It's not for nothing that Toyota ('cheap, reliable cars') launched its luxury car range under a new brand, Lexus, with great success.

5 YOUR EXISTING BRAND IS NOT CREDIBLE TO YOUR NEW TARGET AUDIENCE

The religious, old-fashioned image surrounding the Salvation Army is difficult for young people to connect with. When an idea was developed to create hip new clothes out of old second-hand clothes, it was launched under the brand name 50-50 Originals.

A TRUSTED BRAND IS A GREAT LAUNCH PAD

If the situations as described above don't apply to you, it most probably makes the most sense to launch your new product under your existing brand. This is the most time- and cost-efficient way forward. It empowers you to leverage on trust you have managed to build up with customers and to cross-sell your new product to your current client base and social followers.

USE DESCRIPTORS

To provide clarity to consumers, you can use descriptors to differentiate your products or lines of business from each other. Examples of brands that successfully use this strategy are Virgin and FedEx:

- Virgin Company, Virgin Records, Virgin Atlantic, Virgin Mobile.
- FedEx Corporation, FedEx Express, FedEx Freight, FedEx Ground etc.

Every new product or sub-brand you launch can also strengthen the credibility of your main brand. Google, for example, continually reinforces its innovative and simplifying character with new services like Google Translate, Google Maps, Google Groups etc.

SUB-BRANDS

You can also create a sub-brand (for instance 'Austin Mini' or 'Hilton DoubleTree'), or endorse your new product or company with your corporate brand (for instance 'a Coca-Cola Company'). The latter only makes sense if your current corporate brand has already built up strong trust. If it's not that well known yet, it won't give your new brand extra credibility.

Think before you launch an additional brand. As long as there is a logical relationship or common denominator between different products or services in your portfolio, sticking to one brand is the best investment of your time, money and energy.

Find Suzanne van Gompel at
standoutfromthecrowd.nl
@StandOutFTCrowd

CHAPTER 8
THE BEGINNING

JOIN THE TRIBE

GET SUPPORT FROM PEERS

The brand building process is not easy and you are just getting started. Get support from your peers in our Facebook Group, Brand the Change. Post an ask, join the discussions or share a resource: the tribe brings together a group of experienced changemakers, brand strategists and creatives from across the world. Let's support each other in building the brands we deserve. *www.facebook.com/groups/brandthechange*

HELP US MAKE IT BETTER!

Help this book become the best it can be! Tell us about your experiences using this book. Let us know what is missing, or what we can do more of! What is one thing you would want us to do to make this book better?

SHOW US WHAT YOU'VE CREATED

Share your experience and your outcome with us, and your project might be featured in one of our future case studies, on the website, or via our social media channels.

SUGGEST A CASE STUDY

We are always looking for brands to analyse for the benefit of a case study. We are especially interested in brands from non-Western countries, since these are under-represented in the world's media and educational landscape. Our criteria for a great brand are:

» A unique product or service.
» A differentiating brand strategy.
» A professional visual identity or great name.
» Great brand expressions.

BECOME A TRAINER

Are you a passionate brand strategist, creative, coach or educator and would you like to use our method and tools in your own independent practice?
Join our Trainers Network or Train the Trainers Programme!
Go to www.the-brandling.com/become-a-trainer/

FURTHER READING

Tribe, Seth Godin

Brand Thinking And Other Noble
Pursuits, Debbie Millman

Living the Brand, Nicholas Ind

Traction: How Any Startup Can Achieve
Explosive Customer Growth
Gabriel Weinberg & Justin Mares

Rules for Revolutionaries, How big
organizing can change everything
Becky Bond and Zack Exley

How to, Michael Bierut

Dictionary of Brand, Marty Neumeier

Positioning: The Battle for Your Mind
by Al Ries, Jack Trout

BRAND BUILDING RESOURCES
Acumen+
Online courses in storytelling, marketing
and more
plusacumen.org/courses

Growth Tribe
Amsterdam-based growth hacking
agency offers courses in growth hacking,
a data driven approach to marketing
growthtribe.io

Value Proposition Canvas
Acclaimed canvas to create a compelling
value proposition for your product/
service.
strategyzer.com/canvas/value-
proposition-canvas

Value Proposition Design
Alan Smith, Alexander Osterwalder,
Gregory Bernarda, Trish Papadakos
and Yves Pigneur
strategyzer.com/books/value-
proposition-design

The Story of Self
Worksheet to help build your story by
Marshall Ganz
wholecommunities.org

Solutions Journalism toolkit
solutionsjournalism.org

Common Cause communication,
a toolkit for charities
valuesandframes.org/toolkits

Reframing online tool
reframe.thnk.org

Guide to Facebook for business
facebook.com/business

Basics of Twitter for business
business.twitter.com/basics

Montfort social video guide
montfort.io/social-media-video/

Facebook advertising training
facebook.com/blueprint

Brand New, a blog that reviews
rebranding projects.
underconsideration.com/brandnew

LEGAL MATTERS
Information about trademarks of the
World Intellectual Property Organization
(WIPO) wipo.int/trademarks

Global brand database of WIPO
wipo.int/branddb/en/

Worldwide trademark search
tmdn.org/tmview/welcome

Classification of trademarks
wipo.int/classifications/nice/en/

Links to trademark offices and
classification help
oami.europa.eu/ec2

SOURCES

OVERALL

Cultures and Organisations:
Software of the Mind
*Geert Hofstede, Gert Jan Hofstede,
Michael Minkov*

Business Model Generation
Alexander Osterwalder

Can brands be good? Video
School of Life, Alain de Botton

Reframing, the Art of Thinking
Differently, *Karim Benammar*

The Weird and Ineffable Science of
Naming A Product
Neal Gabler, The New York Times

The Broken 'Buy-One, Give-One'
Model: 3 Ways To Save Tom's Shoes
Cheryl Davenport, FastCoExist

When Mother Teresa Drives
a Ferrari, *D.A. Wallach, Medium.com*

Mapping the Journey
Case 4 Patagonia
Greenleaf Publishing

8 Word Mission Statement
Mulago Foundation

Nike & the Swoosh, *Wikipedia*

Little Book of Values, *IDEO,
Slideshare*

Segmenting audiences at the
base of the pyramid
*V. Kasturi, Rangan Michael & Chu
Djordjija Petkoski, Harvard Business
Review*

How One Startup Developed a Sales
Model That Works in Emerging

Markets
*Jonathan Cedar, Harvard Business
Review*

The problem with the Tata Nano case
Tim Calkins

Tom's shoes, toms.com
Lush, lush.com
Muji, muji.eu
SolarCity, solarcity.com
ColorOfChange, colorofchange.org
Creative Commons
creativecommons.org
Internet of Elephants
internetofelephants.com
Designathon Works
designathonworks.com
Acumen, acumen.org
Nest, nest.com
ClientEarth, clientearth.org
Factory45, factory45.com
SpaceX, spacex.com
Warby Parker, warbyparker.com
MD Anderson Cancer Center
mdanderson.org
Ideo, ideo.com

CASE STUDIES

UK Charity Awareness
Monitor 2004

The Macmillan brand journey
2006–2013
Hillary Cross and Ali Sanders

Macmillan Cancer Support
Wolff Olins
wolffolins.com/work/32/macmillan

Garantie slaafvrije chocolade kan
Tony's nog steeds niet geven
Teun van de Keuken
Volkskrant. 23/10/2015

JaarFAIRslag 2013
Tony's Chocolonely

Headspace app: Meditation
made simple by former monk.
Rebecca Lee, CBS news

How Sugru's inventor knew her idea
would stick.
Brittany Shoot, Fortune

Sugru, the new wonder material: 'I
made a thing like wood, but it
bounced'.
Shane Hickey, The Guardian

Sticky putty Sugru crowdfunds in bid
to rival Sellotape and Blu-Tack
worldwide.
Rebecca Bun-Callander, Telegraph

SuperBetter
Jane McGonigal

The School of life
Alain de Botton
alaindebotton.com/the-school-of-life/

The game that can give you 10 extra
years, *Jane McGonigal*
TED Talk

The Higher Life, a mindfulness guru
for the tech set.
Lizzie Widdicombe, The New Yorker

Interview with Catherine Mahugu
Stephanie Sunderland, ITU News

Branding spotlight: Soko
Allison Doyle, Remake
Sasa Africa Shifts to
ShopSoko.com, Techmoran

Africa's artisans' marketplace Soko
raises $700,000 in early stage round.

Miguel Heilbron, VC4A

Meet the Brooklyn-Born Marine
Biologist Co-Leading the 'March for
Science'
Marina Touré, Observer

Meet the most influential marine
biologist of our time
Stephanie Granada, Outside Online

GUEST ESSAYS

Worksheet 'Telling your public story:
Self, Us, Now' *Marshall Ganz*

Vijf tinten groen. Input voor
effectieve duurzaamheidsstrategieën
*Whitepaper by Motivaction.
M. Hannink, J. Hoekstra & P. P.
Verheggen*

COLOPHON

Author: Anne Miltenburg
Research assistance: Clemence Lagarde, Pauline Taks
Illustrations: Anje Jager

With contributions by: Roshan Paul, Grant Tudor,
Stella van Himbergen, Marleen Splinter, Simon Buckby,
Ben Matthews and Suzanne van Gompel.

Editing: Ted Whang, Anne Miltenburg
Proofreading: Johanna Robinson

Design: The Brandling
DTP: Ton Persoon, Patrick van Gerwen

A big thanks to Ariën Breunis, Raquel Sztejnberg and Max van
Lingen for reading the draft versions of this book and offering
invaluable feedback and suggestions.

A big thank you to our test users: The Amani Institute and
Gautam Shah (Nairobi), Siri Warren (Stockholm), Manuel
Grassler at Fachhochschule der Wirtschaft GmbH and Innolab
(Graz), the global THNK community, Cogite (Tunis), Allynet
(Munich), Mira Gleisberg (Amsterdam) and the team of Alf Khair
(Riyadh).

Thank you Erica Bol (Rewrap), Ronan Hayes (Reflow) and Mark
Janssens (Kibo Bikes) and our 14 case study subjects for
sharing their brand building experiences with our research
team. Your willingness to share your hard-earned lessons will
help others and we need more of that in the world.

I am particularly grateful to THNK (Eduard, Lisa, Mark, Menno,
Bas, Sharon, Bas, Rajiv, Elly, Karim, Betty, Kaz, Lennart,
Mercedes and Berend-Jan) for their inspiration and support
in the development of The Brandling and our tools. An extra big
cheer for Paul van 't Veld, my coach, Auke Ferwerda, my
acceleration mentor and Robert Wolfe, my storytelling trainer.

A special shout out to THNK Class 5 for inspiring me in life,
love, work and beyond and without whom this book would have
never seen the light of day.

No theory can be developed without the practice that my
clients, partners, colleagues and workshop participants provide
me. Shukran, merci, thank you, dank je wel! Juliette
Schraauwers, Reem Khouri, Princess Reema Bint Bandar Al
Saud, AMREF Health Africa (Jackie, Diana), the M-TIBA team
(Felix, Lina, Nicole, Kees), Rym Baouendi, Dr Easkey Britton,
Osher Günsberg, Nivi, Internet of Elephants, Humanity House,
Michael Radke, Gautam Shah, Michael Lang, Adnan Mirza, Emer
Beamer, Patrick van Gerwen, Ellis Bartholomeus, Dr Ayana
Johnson, Alvin Chan, Boyd Coyner, Silo, Jorn Dal, Neil Simmons,
Lotte van Puffelen Palthe, Clever+Franke, Janüska Dawood,
Manon van Paaschen, Jason Eaves, Sidd Goyal, World Economic
Forum, Designathon Works, Demeter Network, the Hult Prize
team and the Amani institute: Roshan Paul and Ila Rabbat.

I am indebted to my 'thuisfront' for its endless support.

KICK STARTER

The first and second edition of this book were published under the title *Branding Toolkit for Changemakers.* Its development was made possible by the generous support of 271 backers from every corner of the world on Kickstarter. Thank you again for your support. Your gift keeps on giving.

MAY LEE
CARLA & WILLEM VERWEIJEN
LIESBETH KRUIZINGA
COLONEL ELANOR BOEKHOLDT-O'SULLIVAN
GAUTAM SHAH
HIMMAT & NIRUPA SHAH
JULIETTE SCHRAAUWERS
KARIN SCHWANDT
EMER BEAMER
JOOST ROOZEKRANS
LENA SLACHMUIJLDER
GUNTER WEHMEYER
HANS VAN DER VLIST
EMMY MILTENBURG
CHANTAL VAN SCHAIK
ANDREAS SAUTTER
CHRIS MILLER
ZIYAD ZALARFA
REEM KHOURI
MADELEINE VAN LENNEP
PETER BIL'AK
DENNIS ELBERS
PATRICK VAN GERWEN
PAUL VAN 'T VELD
LIZA ENEBEIS
INGRID VAN DER WACHT
LEE RAZO
MARGARET ROSE
INEKE MILTENBURG
WILLIAM SACKS
MICHEL DE BOER
DHANANJAY JOSHI
CLINTON DUNCAN
RAJESH DAHIYA
ADNAN MIRZA
EVELINE VELDT

JORN DAL
ELLIS BARTHOLOMEUS
EDWIN SCHMIDHEINY
RYM BAOUENDI
ELODIE BOYER
ZAHLEN TITCOMB
MAUREEN DE JONG
STEFAN SAGMEISTER
AYANA JOHNSON
DARCIE GOODWIN
PASCAL SEEN
ZUIDERLICHT
ADRIAAN MILTENBURG
MARC VAN DER HEIJDE
SYTZE KOOLEN
RENE TONEMAN
STEVE CASSAR
MOULSARI JAIN
MICHAEL LANG
GERT FRANKE
ULLA-BRITT VOGT
SIMON SCHEIBER
OLALLA CASTRO
MIKE RADKE
CEES MENSEN
CORA MOL
KENNETH BRECHER
WISAM AMID
ERIK DE VLAAM
MICHELL ZAPPA
JONS JANSSEN
PAUL VERWEYEN
KEVIN FINN
VINCENT LAZZARA
NASR ALBUSAIDI
RODERICK PERESSO

BERTHA FRENCH
IDA NORRBY
JEROEN VAN ERP
NIVI MUKHERJEE-SHARMA
CASPER PEETERS
ART TO MOVE
TIM BELONAX
AREEJ NAHDI
JOLANDA WILLEMSEN
HATS & TALES
KAMIEL VAN KESSEL
RONALD LENZ
RICK KLAAIJSEN
VIMALA PALANISWAMY
MICHEL BACHMANN
VERA JANSEN
THIJS DE BOER
FRANKLIN DE BEKKER
30 WEEKS
THOMAS DAHM
MERLIJN TWAALFHOVEN
GUUS BOUDESTEIN
PABLA VAN HECK
INGE NIKS
JEMMA LAND
KEITH BROCK
JOHN MONKS
MANUEL GRASSLER
HEIDE GORIS
JESSY KATE SCHINGLER
STRAYBULLETS
PIET-HEIN HERFKENS
MARCIS VANADZINS
TOBIAS TIEFERT
BILL HUB
MARIEKE BROMMERSMA

MATTEO BARTOLI
DANIELA KRAUTSACK
MARCEL KAMPMAN
STEPHEN BRITTAIN
MAX VAN LINGEN
MARIAN COUNIHAN
MARIT TURK
STEPHAN EGLOFF
RUBEN COLLIN
DANIEL S. LEE
DAVE NEETSON
SAYFEDINE BOUHLEL
NEAL GORENFLO
SHARON CHANG
MICHAEL GILMORE
LESTHER VAN VLIET
LISA RING VAN EEK
WOLFGANG RUBER
SHAREEFA FADHEL
ACE THANABOON
SOMBOON
MARCO-PAUL DE JEU
NEIL SIMMONS
SIERDJAN WESTEN
STEFAN RUISSEN
DYLAN GRIFFITH
SEAN DEEKS
SEBASTIAN BANCK
HWIE-BING KWEE